making children's clothes

making
children's
clothes

25 stylish step-by-step sewing
projects for 0–5 years

EMMA HARDY

CICO BOOKS
LONDON NEW YORK

Published in 2009 by CICO Books
An imprint of Ryland Peters & Small Ltd

20–21 Jockey's Fields   519 Broadway, 5th Floor
London WC1R 4BW   New York, NY 10012

www.cicobooks.com

10 9 8 7 6 5 4 3 2 1

Text © Emma Hardy 2009
Design and photography © CICO Books 2009

A CIP catalog record for this book is available from the Library
of Congress and the British Library.

ISBN-13: 978 1 906525 79 8

Editor: Sarah Hoggett
Designer: Roger Hammond @ bluegumdesigners.com
Illustrator: Michael Hill
Photographer: Vanessa Davies
Pattern cutter: Bernadette Thornton
Printed in China

DEDICATION
For my Nana, Alice Nicol, whose sewing skills have inspired
several generations of our family.

ACKNOWLEDGMENTS
Thank you to Vanessa Davies for the beautiful photography, to
Michael Hill for making the steps look so lovely and to Sarah
Hoggett for making sense of it all.

I am indebted to Bernadette Thornton who worked so hard
cutting the patterns and offered so much help and support
throughout the project. Thank you Bernie.

Thank you to our gorgeous models—Freya Bartlett, Jonathan
Hadfield, and Betty Dahl. And thank you to Kate Wheeler, Ben
Bartlett, and Trish Harrington for having such lovely children.

Thank you to Cindy Richards for the opportunity to do this book
and to Pete Jorgensen and Sally Powell for the help and support.

And of course thank you to my lovely family, Laurie, Gracie, and
Betty who make it all possible.

contents

Introduction 6

BABYWEAR 1
Baby booties 8

Baby's bib 12

Baby's hat 16

TOPS & SMOCKS 2
Petal top 20

Smock top 24

Sleeveless top 28

Boy's shirt 32

PANTS & SHORTS 3
Elasticated pants 36

Boy's shorts 40

Capri pants 44

Baby bloomers 48

SKIRTS & DRESSES 4
Corduroy skirt 52

Puffball skirt 56

Gypsy skirt 60

Pinafore dress 62

Toddler's dress 66

Party dress 70

SLEEPWEAR 5
Pajamas 74

Dressing gown 80

Nightdress 84

ACCESSORIES 6
Apron 88

Double-sided hat 92

Scarf 96

Poncho 100

Hairband 102

Techniques 104

Templates 109

Suppliers 110

Index 112

How to use the pull-out patterns 112

introduction

There is something very satisfying about sewing clothes for your own and for friends' children. Store-bought clothes, which can be bought so cheaply these days, are often of inferior quality and can be covered in logos and branding—so why not make them yourself?

The idea of this book is to provide you with a basic collection of easy-to-make, but stylish children's clothes that you can customize and embellish to create one-off garments for your little ones. All the patterns are suitable for the novice stitcher as well as the more experienced seamstress. They require only small pieces of fabric—and none of the projects will take longer than an afternoon to finish.

The book is split into chapters, with garments for babies and toddlers alongside clothes for children between 2 and 5 years. Lots of the projects are unisex, and look great in a wide range of fabrics. I have included ideas for some lovely finishing touches, like fabric flowers and bow decorations, which can be used in lots of different ways and mixed and matched with different projects.

Each project has a list of materials including a fabric quantity, which is based on the largest pattern size for that garment. All the measurements are given in imperial and metric sizes: it is important to stick to either one or the other when following the instructions. The sizes of the patterns are also listed; again, it is a good idea to follow the instructions and measurements for each size, although obviously hems and arm lengths can easily be altered. Bear in mind that children grow quickly—so check the size chart below before you start to work out which size would be best. There is nothing worse than lovingly creating something to find that it does not fit!

With such a wide selection of fabrics available, both from stores and also on-line, you can have lots of fun making things in your and your children's favorite designs and colors, personalizing things to make them really special. Once you start making children's clothes, you will realize just how quick and easy they are. You will never want to go clothes shopping again! Happy sewing!

Size Chart

	6–12 months	12–24 months	2–3 years	3–4 years	4–5 years
HEIGHT	29 in./76 cm	32¹/₂ in./83 cm	38¹/₂ in./98 cm	41 in./104 cm	43¹/₂ in./110 cm
CHEST	18¹/₂ in./47 cm	19 in./48 cm	20¹/₂ in./52 cm	22 in./56 cm	23 in./58 cm
WAIST	17¹/₂ in./44 cm	18 in./46 cm	19¹/₂ in./50 cm	20¹/₂ in./52 cm	21¹/₂ in./54 cm

Baby booties

These adorable booties will keep toes cozy as well as looking cute! Made from linen, which holds its shape well but is still soft and flexible, they are lined with contrasting fabric and finished with decorative buttons. Snap fasteners are used on the straps, making it easy to put the booties on and take them off.

You will need

* Pattern pieces 5 and 6 from the pull-out section and template on page 110

* 32 x 8 in. (80 x 20 cm) each of two contrasting fabrics

* 32 x 8 in. (80 x 20 cm) iron-on interfacing

* 2 snap fasteners

* 2 buttons, approx. ³/₄ in. (2 cm) in diameter, or ready-made fabric flower

SIZES

The patterns are for ages 0–3 months and 3–9 months.

Take ¹/₂-in. (1-cm) seam allowances throughout, unless otherwise stated.

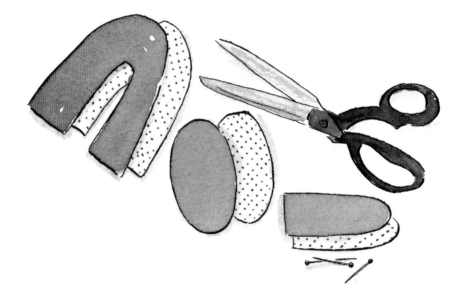

I Using pattern pieces 5 and 6 from the pull-out sheets provided and the strap pattern on page 110, cut out two soles, two uppers, and two straps from each of the two fabrics, remembering to flip the patterns so that you have a right and a left foot. Using the same pattern pieces, cut out interfacing for the soles, uppers, and straps.

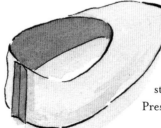

2 Following the manufacturer's instructions, iron the interfacing to the wrong side of the outer bootie pieces. With right sides together, pin and machine stitch the back seams on the outer uppers. Press the seams open.

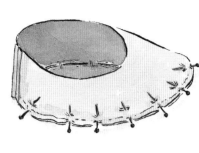
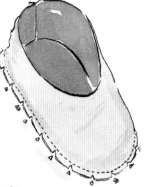
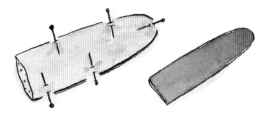

3 With right sides together, pin and baste (tack) the uppers to the soles. Machine stitch them together, and remove the basting (tacking) stitches. Make small snips in the seam allowance all the way around.

4 With right sides together, machine stitch the outer and lining strap pieces together, leaving the end open. Trim the seam allowance, and turn right side out. Press.

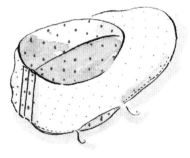
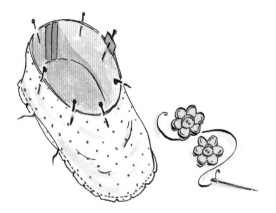

5 Pin and stitch the back seam of the lining uppers, as in Step 2, and press the seams open. Pin and baste (tack) the lining uppers to the sole linings, leaving a small opening of about 1 in. (2.5 cm). Snip the seam allowance all the way around, and press.

6 With right sides together, slip the lining over the outer bootie, inserting the strap inside the seam in the correct position. Machine stitch all the way around. Turn right side out, through the opening in the lining, and slipstitch the opening closed (see page 105). Hand stitch a snap fastener to the underside of each strap and in the corresponding place on the bootie. Sew a button or bow to the front of the strap to decorate.

TIPS
Make these cute booties in checked and striped fabrics for baby boys, choosing suitable colors and buttons. For girls, stitch bows onto the straps instead of buttons for a really pretty finish.

Baby's bib

Thick toweling fabric, readily available from fabric stores, makes these charming bibs super soft and very absorbent. Alternatively, you could cut up store-bought towels, which are available in a wide range of colors. Add a personal touch with an appliquéd fruit motif, using scraps of patterned fabrics in bright colors. Remember to choose cotton fabrics that can be laundered at high temperatures for the appliqué.

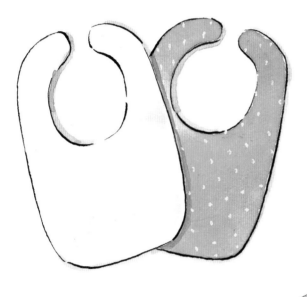

I Using pattern piece 24 from the pull-out sheets provided, make a paper pattern (see page 104) for the bib. Cut out one piece from toweling and one from the backing fabric.

2 Using the templates on pages 109–III, make paper patterns for your chosen appliqué motif. Following the manufacturer's instructions, iron fusible bonding web to the back of the fabric scraps. Draw the motifs on the back of the fabric scraps and cut out.

You will need

* *Pattern piece 24 from the pull-out section and templates on pages 109–111*

* *12 x 16 in. (30 x 40 cm) toweling fabric*

* *12 x 16 in. (30 x 40 cm) backing fabric, plus a piece at least 28 in. (70 cm) square for binding*

* *Scraps of fabric at least 4 in. (10 cm) square for appliqué*

* *Approx. 8 in. (20 cm) square of fusible bonding web for each appliqué design*

* *Hook-and-loop tape, 1 in. (2.5 cm) square*

SIZE

The finished bib measures approx. 13½ x 9½ in. (34 x 24 cm).

Take ½-in. (1-cm) seam allowances throughout, unless otherwise stated.

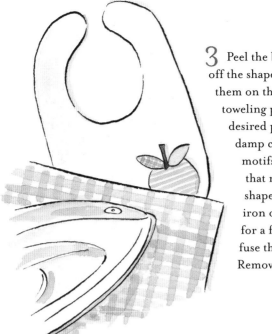

3 Peel the backing paper off the shapes and lay them on the front of the toweling piece in the desired place. Lay a damp cloth over the motifs, making sure that none of the shapes move, and iron over the cloth for a few seconds to fuse the fabrics. Remove the cloth.

4 Machine stitch all around the shapes, stitching as close to the edges as possible. Trim all of the thread ends neatly.

5 Wrong sides together, lay the toweling piece on the backing piece. Baste (tack) the pieces together (see page 105).

6 From the backing fabric, cut a 57 x 1½-in. (145 x 4-cm) strip of fabric on the bias (see page 107). Press ⅜ in. (1 cm) under to the wrong side at one end. With right sides together, pin and stitch the strip around the toweling piece, overlapping the ends a little.

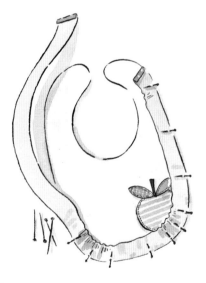

7 Trim the seam allowance all the way around the bib. Press 3/8 in. (1 cm) under to the wrong side all the way along the bias strip. Pin this folded edge to the back of the bib. Slipstitch it in place all the way around (see page 105).

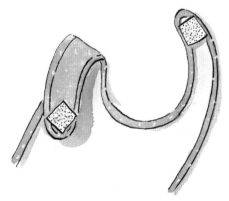

8 Pin and stitch the hook side of a piece of hook-and-loop tape to the underside of one end of the bib and the loop side to the upper side of the other end.

Baby's hat

This super-cute hat is so quick and easy to make, and will keep baby warm and cozy, too. Make it in soft jersey fabric in pretty pastel colors or fun stripes, with a coordinating fabric for the ears. If you can't get hold of jersey fabric on the roll, cut up a store-bought T-shirt.

You will need

* *Templates on pages 109–111*
* *16 x 24 in. (40 x 60 cm) T-shirt or stretchy jersey fabric*
* *4-in. (10-cm) square scrap of coordinating fabric for inner ears*
* *4-in. (10-cm) square of fusible bonding web*
* *20 in. (50 cm) ribbon, ⅛ in. (3 mm) wide*

SIZE

The finished hat is approx. 5½ in. (14 cm) tall and 16 in. (41 cm) in circumference.

Take ½-in. (1-cm) seam allowances throughout, unless otherwise stated.

I Using the template on page 109, cut out the two hat pieces from stretchy jersey or T-shirt fabric. Pin the pattern securely onto the fabric, as stretchy fabric can move when it is being cut. With right sides together, pin and machine stitch the two hat pieces together. Trim the seam allowance to about ¼ in. (5 mm) and make small snips in the seam allowance at the bottom of the ears, taking care not to cut into the stitching.

2 Following the manufacturer's instructions, iron fusible bonding web to the back of the scrap of fabric for the inner ears. Using the template on page 111, cut out two inner ear shapes.

4 Topstitch around the inner ears, stitching as close to the edge as possible, starting and finishing the stitching at the bottom (which will not show when the ribbon is tied in place). This will help them to stand out and keep their shape.

3 Turn the hat right side out and press, making sure that the ears have a neat curve. Position the inner ears on the hat, peel off the backing papers, lay a damp cloth over the fabric, and press down for a few seconds with a medium-hot iron to fuse the inner ears in place.

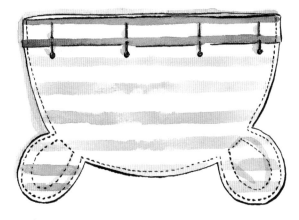

5 Turn the hat wrong side out. Turn over the bottom edge to the wrong side by 3/8 in. (1 cm) and then by another 3/4 in. (2 cm). Pin and machine stitch all the way around, stitching as close to the first fold line as possible. Make sure that you do not stretch the fabric while sewing. Press.

6 Cut two 10-in. (25-cm) lengths of ribbon. Tie them tightly around the base of the ears in a bow. Trim the ends of the ribbons neatly.

Petal top

This stylish little top is so easy to make and, as it uses only two pattern pieces, it can be finished in no time. Made from a lightweight cotton fabric, it looks great worn over a plain, long-sleeved T-shirt or on its own as a pretty summer top. A slightly longer version would make a lovely kaftan for beachwear.

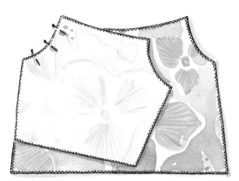

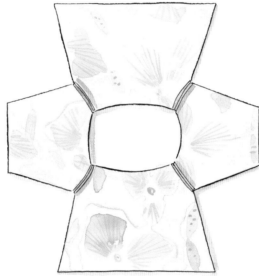

I Using pattern pieces 3 and 19 from the pull-out sheets provided, cut out two body pieces and two sleeve pieces from the main fabric. Overlock or zigzag (see page 106) along all sides of all four pieces. Lay one of the sleeve pieces on one of the body pieces, right sides together, aligning the curves exactly. Pin and machine stitch along the curve. Press the seam open.

2 Stitch the other sleeve piece to the other side of the same body piece in the same way, then pin and machine stitch the second body piece to the other side of the sleeve pieces, as illustrated. Press the seams open.

You will need

* Pattern pieces 3 and 19 from the pull-out section

* 45 x 40 in. (115 x 100 cm) fabric

* 1 yd (1 m) ribbon, ¼ in. (6 mm) wide

* 44 in. (110 cm) elastic, ¼ in. (6 mm) wide

* 4 x 12½ in. (10 x 32 cm) each of two coordinating fabrics for flower

SIZES

The patterns are for ages 2–3, 3–4, and 4–5 years.

Take ½-in. (1-cm) seam allowances throughout, unless otherwise stated.

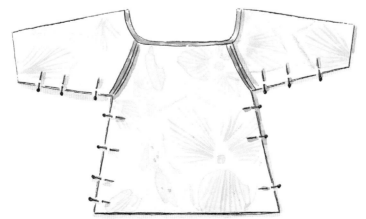

3 With right sides together, pin and machine stitch the sides of the body and both underarm seams. Press the seams open.

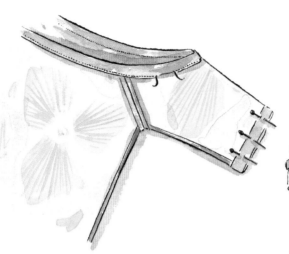

4 Turn under ³/₈ in. (I cm) and then another ³/₈ in. (I cm) to the wrong side around the neck and both sleeves. Pin and machine stitch in place, sewing as close to the edge of the fold as you can, leaving a small opening of about ³/₄ in. (2 cm) on each hem to form channels for the elastic.

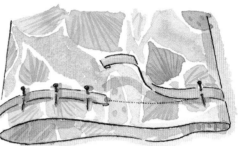

5 Along the bottom edge, turn under ¹/₂ in. (I cm) and then another ³/₄ in. (2 cm) to the wrong side and machine stitch in place. Pin and machine stitch a length of ribbon over this stitching line on the right side, sewing as close to the edges of the ribbon as you can. Overlap the ends of the ribbon and turn the ends under a little for a neat finish.

6 Cut one 24-in. (60-cm) and two IO-in. (25-cm) lengths of elastic (check the length on the child first; you will need slightly less for smaller sizes). Using a safety pin, feed the elastic through the channels in the neck and arms (see page 108). Machine stitch the ends of the elastic together, then machine stitch the openings closed.

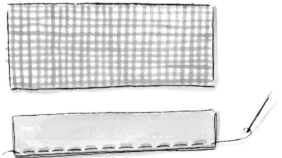

7 With right sides together, fold each strip of coordinating fabric for the flower in half widthwise, then pin and machine stitch along the length. Turn right side out and press. Turn both ends into the wrong side by about ¹/₂ in. (I cm) and slipstitch neatly in place (see page 105).

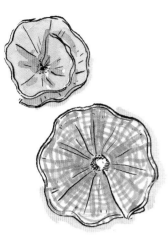

8 Work a line of a running stitch
along one long edge of each piece
and gather slightly (see page 106).
Roll the two strips around each
other to form a flower and stitch
them securely together.

9 Hand stitch the flower to the
top, using small, neat stitches to
hold it in place.

Smock top

This gorgeous smock-style top looks more complicated to make than it is. Sewing the elastic in place takes a little practice, but it is not difficult, and the end result is certainly worth the effort. Try out the technique on a scrap of fabric before you start. Great as a sun top, this top also looks good worn over a T-shirt. Alternatively, make a longer version as a pretty summer dress.

You will need

* *Template on page 110*
* *36 x 18 in. (91 x 44 cm) main fabric*
* *44 x 4 in. (110 x 10 cm) fabric for the border and pocket*
* *72 in. (180 cm) elastic, ⅛ in. (3 mm) wide*
* *Air-soluble marker pen*

SIZES

The patterns are for ages 2–3, 3–4, and 4–5 years.

Take ½-in. (1-cm) seam allowances throughout, unless otherwise stated.

I Cut a 9½ x 34½-in./24 x 87-cm (12 x 35-in./30 x 89-cm: 14½ x 35½-in./36 x 91-cm) rectangle of fabric. Turn under ⅜ in. (1 cm) and then another ⅜ in. (1 cm) to the wrong side along one long edge. Pin and machine stitch in place, stitching as close to the last fold as possible. Press.

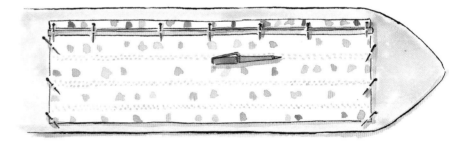

2 Cut three 24-in. (60-cm) lengths of elastic. Baste (tack) the end of one piece to the left of the fabric, on the wrong side just under the top fold. Lay the fabric flat on an ironing board. Pin it to the board at both ends to hold the fabric firmly in place. Insert pins across the fabric at 6-in. (15-cm) intervals. Stretch the elastic to the right-hand side in a straight line and make a pen mark on the elastic at each pin. Un-pin the fabric. Using a small zigzag stitch (see page 106), machine stitch the elastic, stretching it so that the pen marks line up with the pins and pulling the top end of the fabric taut as you go.

3 Baste (tack) the second piece of elastic to the left-hand edge of the fabric as before, about 5/8 in. (1.5 cm) below the first. Pin the fabric onto the ironing board so that it is taut again, and repeat the marking and stitching process. Sew a third piece of elastic in place, 5/8 in. (1.5 cm) below the second, in the same way.

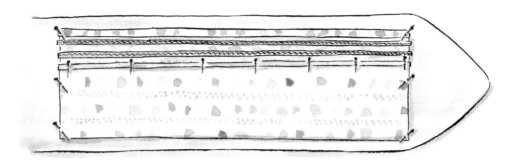

4 Cut a piece of border fabric 3¼ in. (8 cm) deep and 34½ in./87 cm (35 in./89 cm: 35½ in./91 cm) wide. With right sides together, pin and machine stitch the border to the bottom edge of the main piece, aligning the raw edges. Press the seam toward the bottom edge. With right sides together, pin and stitch the side edges together, then overlock or zigzag stitch the raw edges together.

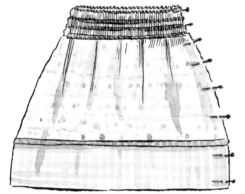

5 Cut two 10 x 3¼-in. (25 x 8-cm) pieces of the main fabric for the straps. Turn under 3/8 in. (1 cm) on all four sides of both pieces to the wrong side and press. With wrong sides together, fold the strips in half, pin, and topstitch all the way around. Try the top on the child, and pin and stitch the straps in place to the required length on the inside of the top.

6 Turn under 3/8 in. (1 cm) to the wrong side along the bottom raw edge and press. Align this fold with the top of the border on the inside of the top, pin, and hand stitch in place.

7 Using the heart template on page 110, make a paper pattern (see page 104). Cut two pocket pieces from the border fabric. (You could line the pocket with the main fabric if you wish.) With right sides together, pin and machine stitch the pieces together, leaving a small opening of about ¾ in. (2 cm) along one straight edge. Trim the seam allowance slightly and make small snips in the curved areas. Turn right side out and topstitch all the way around.

8 Pin and stitch the pocket onto the front of the top, as shown, leaving the top open. Make a few forward and reverse stitches at the ends of the stitching lines to give extra strength. Press.

Sleeveless top

The bright bold print used on this cotton top is edged with a simple spotted fabric, with an oversized bow providing beautiful detailing. With a button fastening at the back, this is a very easy garment to make. It could, of course, be made without the bow decoration for an easy-to-wear, everyday top.

1 Using pattern pieces 34 and 36 from the pull-out sheets provided, cut out one front and two back pieces from the main fabric. Overlock or zigzag stitch (see page 106) along the vertical sides of all three pieces. With right sides together, pin and machine stitch the back pieces to the front at the shoulders. Press the seams open.

2 With right sides together, pin and machine stitch the sides together. Press the seams open.

You will need

* *Pattern pieces 34 and 36 from the pull-out section*

* *44 x 18 in. (110 x 45 cm) main fabric*

* *44 x 22 in. (110 x 55 cm) binding fabric*

* *4 medium snap fasteners*

* *4 buttons, 3/4 in. (2 cm) in diameter*

SIZES

The patterns are for ages 2–3, 3–4, and 4–5 years.

Take 1/2-in. (1-cm) seam allowances throughout, unless otherwise stated.

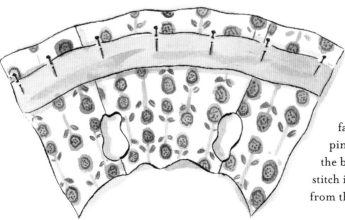

3 Cut a 4 3/4 x 23-in (12 x 58-cm) strip of the binding fabric. With right sides together, pin the binding 1 1/2 in. (4 cm) from the bottom edge of the top. Machine stitch it to the top, stitching 2 in. (5 cm) from the bottom edge.

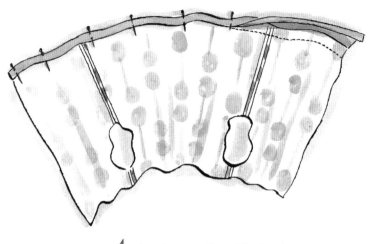

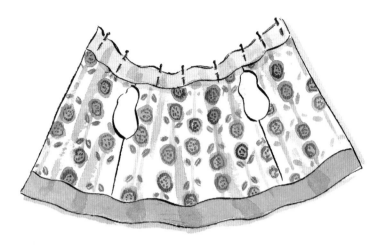

4 On the raw edge of the binding strip, press 3/8 in. (1 cm) to the wrong side. Fold the binding over to the wrong side of the top, aligning the folded edge with the machine stitching on the right side. Pin, then slipstitch it in place (see page 105). Press.

5 Cut strips of the binding fabric 1½ in. (4 cm) wide on the bias (see page 107). Pin one strip to the right side of the top around the neck. Machine stitch it in place. Press 3/8 in. (1 cm) to the wrong side along the long raw edge of the binding strip. Pin and slipstitch it to the wrong side of the top. Press.

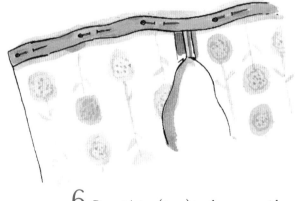

6 Press 3/8 in. (1 cm) to the wrong side along the long raw edge of the binding strip. Pin and slipstitch it to the wrong side of the top. Press.

7 With right sides together, aligning the raw edges, pin and machine stitch binding around the armholes, folding under 3/8 in. (1 cm) at one end of both strips. Turn under 3/8 in. (1 cm) along the raw edge of the strips, as with the neck binding, and slipstitch to the wrong side of the top.

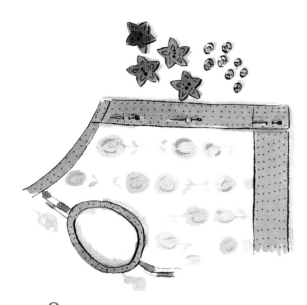

8 Along both raw back edges, press 3/8 in. (1 cm) to the wrong side. Turn under by another 1¼ in. (3 cm). Pin and machine stitch close to the first fold. Sew snap fasteners onto the back edges, as shown on the pattern piece, with a button over each one.

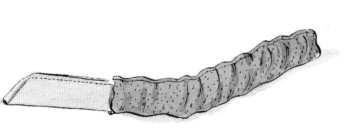

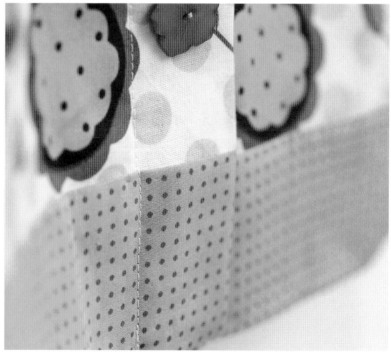

9 Cut a 31½ x 2½-in. (80 x 6.5-cm) strip of fabric for the bow. Fold it in half widthwise, right sides together. Pin and machine stitch along one short end at an angle and along the long edge. Trim the corners and turn right side out. Press and turn under 3/8 in. (1 cm) at the open end, again at an angle, and slipstitch closed. Tie in to a neat bow and stitch in place on the front of the top.

Boy's shirt

This simple shirt, with patch pockets in a contrasting fabric, has a delightfully old-fashioned feel but looks great when worn with jeans or combat pants. It is a classic style that will work in lots of different fabrics, from bright and busy patterns to crisp checks and ginghams.

You will need

* Pattern pieces 8, 14, 25, and 28 from the pull-out section
* 36 x 40 in. (92 x 102 cm) main fabric
* Scrap of contrasting fabric for pockets
* 4 buttons, ¾ in. (2 cm) in diameter

SIZES

The patterns are for ages 2–3, 3–4, and 4–5 years.

Take ½-in. (1-cm) seam allowances throughout, unless otherwise stated.

1 Using pattern pieces 25 and 28 from the pull-out sheets provided, cut out one back piece and two front pieces. Overlock or zigzag stitch around the side edges, armholes, and shoulders. With right sides together, pin and machine stitch the fronts to the back along the shoulders. Press the seams open.

2 Using pattern piece 14 from the pull-out sheet, cut out two sleeve pieces. With right sides together, pin the sleeves around the armholes, easing the sleeve pieces around the curves. Machine stitch. Press the seams toward the arms.

3 With right sides together, pin and machine stitch the underarm and side seams together, making sure the front and back align at the armhole seam. Press the seams open.

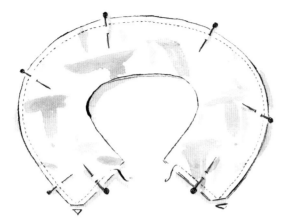

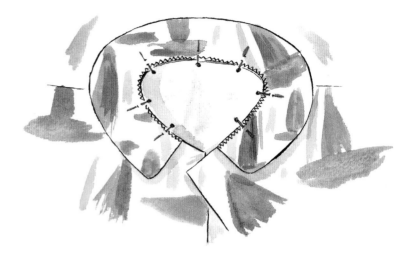

4 Using pattern piece 8 from the pull-out sheet, cut out two collar pieces. With right sides together, pin and machine stitch them together around the outer edges, stopping 3/8 in. (1 cm) before the inner edge at each side. Snip the corners and trim the seam allowance. Turn right side out and press.

5 Overlock or zigzag stitch around the raw edge of the collar, stitching through both layers. Pin the collar around the neck of the shirt on the right side, making sure that it is positioned centrally, and stitch in place.

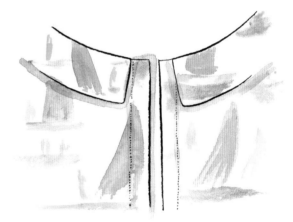

6 Turn the front edges to the wrong side by 3/8 in. (1 cm), pin, and machine stitch in place. Turn both edges to the right side by 1 1/4 in. (3 cm) and machine stitch across the top. Turn right side out to form a neat corner at the top.

7 Press the fronts of the shirt to form a placket 1 1/4 in. (3 cm) wide on each side. Topstitch the plackets in place.

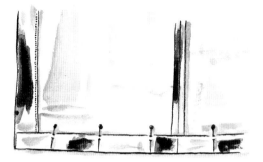

8 Turn the bottom edge of the shirt to the wrong side by ³/₈ in. (I cm) and then by another ³/₈ in. (I cm), and pin in place. Machine stitch. Repeat on both cuffs. Press.

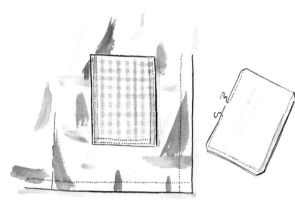

9 Cut two 8³/₄ x 4¹/₂-in. (22 x 11-cm) rectangles of pocket fabric. Fold each one in half, with right sides together, and pin and stitch around the three open sides, leaving an opening of about I in. (2.5 cm) along one side. Snip the corners and turn right side out. Press. Position the pockets on the front of the shirt, about 2 in. (5 cm) from the bottom edge, and pin them in place, with the folded edge forming the top of the pocket. Topstitch around three sides, leaving the top edge open, with one line of stitching as close to the edge as possible and another line just below it. Press.

10 Mark the position and stitch the buttonholes (see page 108). Snip the buttonholes open carefully. Stitch the buttons onto the other placket in the correct position.

PANTS & SHORTS 3
Elasticated pants

This basic pattern can be adapted to make pants in lots of different styles, suitable for both boys and girls. Make them shorter for summer wear, or take in the sides to create a more tapered look, and add pockets in a coordinating fabric that are both practical and decorative.

You will need

* Pattern pieces 15 and 30 from the pull-out section
* 56 x 36 in. (142 x 90 cm) main fabric
* Scraps of fabric for pockets and tie
* 26 in. (65 cm) bias binding
* 23 in. (58 cm) elastic, 1/2 in. (13 mm) wide

SIZES

The patterns are for ages 2–3, 3–4, and 4–5 years.

Take 1/2-in. (1-cm) seam allowances throughout, unless otherwise stated.

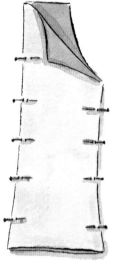

I Using pattern pieces 15 and 30 from the pull-out sheets provided, cut out two front and two back pieces, making sure that there are two left and two right leg pieces. Overlock or zigzag stitch along the outer edges of each piece. With right sides together, pin and machine stitch the left front and back pieces together along the outer edge, and then the inner leg. Repeat with the right leg pieces. Press the seams open.

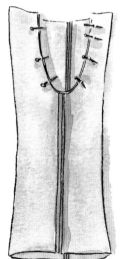

2 Turn one leg right side out and slip it inside the other leg, so that the right sides are together. Pin together, aligning the inner and outer seams on both legs, and machine stitch around the crotch. Trim the seam allowance to 1/4 in. (5 mm) and overlock or zigzag stitch around it.

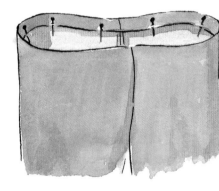

3 Turn over 3/8 in. (1 cm) and then another 3/4 in. (2 cm) to the wrong side along the top edge. Pin and machine stitch close to the bottom fold, leaving an opening of about 1 in. (2.5 cm) at the back. (This forms the channel for the elastic.) Press.

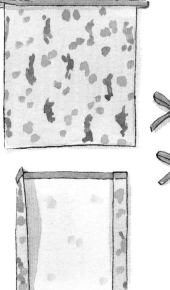

4 Cut two 5½ x 4¾-in. (14 x 12-cm) rectangles of pocket fabric. Cut two pieces of bias binding the width of the pockets. Pin and machine stitch one strip across the top of each pocket. Tie a small bow from bias binding and hand stitch it onto the middle of the pocket top. Fold over ⅜ in. (1 cm) to the wrong side along the pocket sides.

5 Pin and topstitch the pockets onto the front of the pants.

6 To make the tie, cut an 18 x 1½-in. (45 x 4-cm) strip of the pocket fabric and fold it in half along the length. Fold over ⅜ in. (1 cm) at each short end. Fold each long side of the strip in to the center, press, pin, and topstitch all around.

7 Thread the elastic through the waist channel, secure the elastic, and machine stitch the opening closed (see page 108). Check the length of the pants and hem the legs by folding under ⅜ in. (1 cm) and then another ¾ in. (2 cm) to the inside. Press, pin, and machine stitch in place, stitching as close to the last fold as possible. Hand stitch a bow made from the tie from the previous step onto the front, below the elastic.

Boy's shorts

These shorts are practical and look great, too. Clothes for boys can be a little dull, so use a brightly patterned fabric for the turn-ups and pocket linings to make them more fun. Choose fabrics that will withstand a fair amount of wear and tear and make large roomy pockets that are ideal for storing treasured collections.

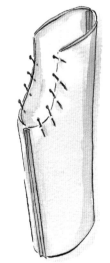

1 Using pattern pieces 2 and 7 from the pull-out sheets provided, cut out two front and two back pieces. (Make sure that there are two left and two right leg pieces.) Overlock or zigzag stitch along the inner and outer edges, from the waist to the bottom of the leg, on all four pieces. With right sides together, pin and machine stitch the left front to the left back along the outer edge and then along the inner leg. Repeat with the right front and back pieces. Press the seams open.

You will need

* Pattern pieces 2 and 7 from the pull-out section

* 48 x 24 in. (120 x 60 cm) main fabric

* 38 x 14 in. (96 x 36 cm) contrasting fabric

* 20 in. (50 cm) elastic, 3/4 in. (2 cm) wide

* 2 buttons, 5/8 in. (15 mm) in diameter

SIZES

The patterns are for ages 2–3, 3–4, and 4–5 years.

Take 1/2-in. (1-cm) seam allowances throughout, unless otherwise stated.

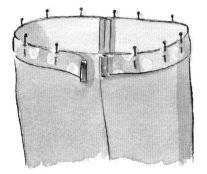

2 Turn one leg right side out and slip it inside the other leg, so that the right sides are together. Pin and machine stitch the two legs together around the crotch, aligning the tops of the legs exactly. Turn right side out.

3 Cut a 2 x 26-in./5 x 66-cm (2 x 28³/₈-in./5 x 72-cm: 2 x 30³/₄-in./5 x 78-cm) strip of contrasting fabric. Fold over ³/₈ in. (1 cm) to the wrong side at both short ends and press. Pin and machine stitch the strip around the top of the shorts, with right sides together, aligning the ends with the back seam.

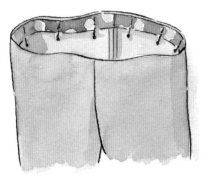

4 Press the contrasting strip over to the inside of the shorts and turn under to the wrong side by 3/8 in. (1 cm). Machine stitch in place, stitching as close to the edge of the fabric as you can. Topstitch around the top of the waist.

5 Cut two 4³/₄ x 16¹/₂-in/12 x 42-cm (4³/₄ x 15³/₄-in./12 x 40-cm: 4³/₄ x 16¹/₂-in/12 x 42-cm) rectangles of contrasting fabric for the bottom cuffs. With right sides together, fold the rectangles in half widthwise, and stitch down the side to form a tube. Turn the shorts inside out. With right sides together, aligning the raw edges, pin and machine stitch each tube to the bottom of one leg.

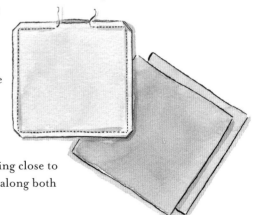

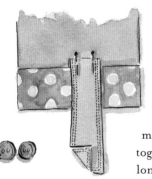

6 Turn the shorts right side out. Pull the bottom cuffs out, turn under 3/8 in. (1 cm) to the wrong side, and press. Pin this folded edge onto the bottom of the leg, in line with the stitch line from Step 5, and machine stitch. Press.

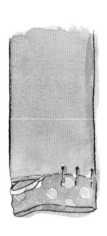

7 Cut two 4¹/₄ x 2¹/₄-in. (11 x 5.5-cm) rectangles from the main fabric and two from the contrasting fabric. With right sides together, pin and machine stitch one of each fabric together around one short and two long sides, leaving one short end unstitched. Snip the corners (see page 106) and turn right side out. Topstitch two rows of stitches all around each one. Fold one end of each flap over by 3/4 in. (2 cm), pin, and machine stitch to the inside of the legs, in line with the stitching of the cuff on the outer side. Turn the shorts right side out, fold up the bottom cuff, and sew a button onto the flap to hold it in place.

8 Cut two 6³/₄ x 6-in./17 x 15-cm (7¹/₄ x 6¹/₂ in./18.5 x 16.5-cm: 8 x 7-in./20 x 18-cm) rectangles from the main fabric and two from the contrasting fabric. With right sides together, pin and machine stitch one of each piece together, leaving a small opening. Snip the corners and turn right side out. Press. Topstitch two lines of stitching along the top of each pocket, and one line 3/8 in. (1 cm) in from the edge around the other three sides. Position the pockets on the legs, as indicated on the pattern piece, and topstitch in place, sewing close to the edge of the pocket along both sides and the bottom.

9 To make the pocket flaps, cut two 6³/₄ x 2³/₈-in./17 x 6-cm (7¹/₄ x 3-in./18.5 x 8.5-cm: 8 x 3⁵/₈-in./20 x 9-cm) rectangles from the main fabric and two from the contrasting fabric. With right sides together, pin and machine stitch one of each piece together along both short ends and one long side, making a slight curve at each end. Snip off the corners and turn right side out. Topstitch around the three sides that you've just machined. Turn under ³/₈ in. (1 cm) along the unstitched side, and position on the shorts just above the pockets. Topstitch across the top of the flap just below the top edge and again about ¹/₂ in. (just over 1 cm) below.

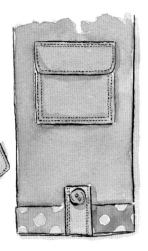

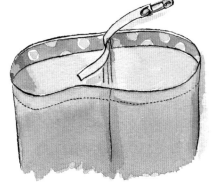

10 Thread the elastic through the waist channel, secure the elastic, and slipstitch the opening closed (see page 108). Press.

Capri pants

These lovely Capri pants, made from a pretty vintage-looking fabric, have a real retro feel. The flat front gives a smart, tailored look, with elastic around the back ensuring a neat and comfortable fit. To make shorts in the same style, simply shorten the legs to the required length and hem the bottoms—or add a frill, as described here.

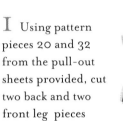

I Using pattern pieces 20 and 32 from the pull-out sheets provided, cut two back and two front leg pieces from the main fabric, making sure that there are two left and two right leg pieces. Overlock or zigzag stitch along the outer edges. Using pattern piece I, cut two waistband pieces. With right sides together, pin and stitch the waistband pieces together along the center fronts. Snip the seam allowance at the center, and press.

2 With right sides together, pin and machine stitch the fronts to the backs along the inner seam. Press the seam open.

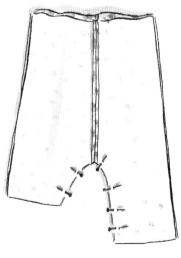

3 With right sides together, pin and machine stitch the legs together, aligning the crotch and seams.

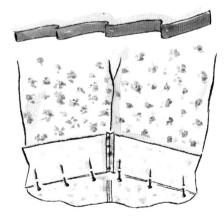

4 With right sides together, pin and stitch the waistband to the front of the pants, aligning the raw edges. Fold the waistband up along the stitching line, so that it's right side out, and press. Pin and machine stitch the ribbon over the waistband seam.

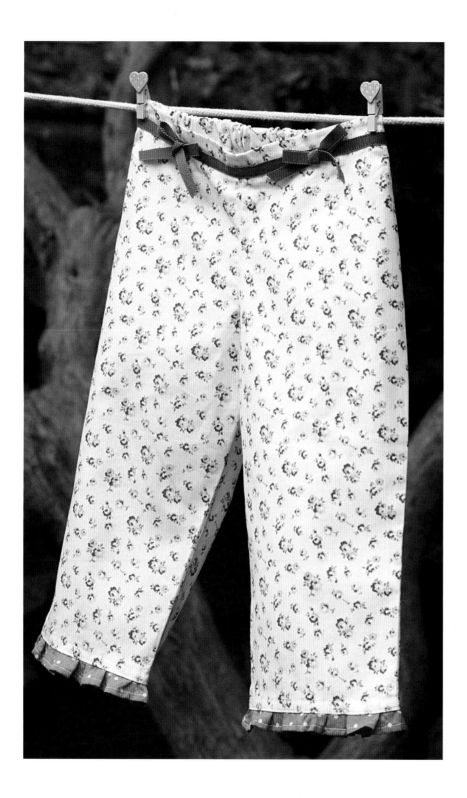

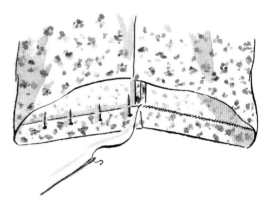

5   With right sides together, pin and machine stitch the outer leg seams. Press the seams open.

6   Along the raw edge of the front waistband, fold under ⅜ in. (I cm) and then another ¾ in. (2 cm) to the wrong side. Pin and slipstitch (see page 105) the front waistband in place along the stitch line from Step 4. Make two bows from grosgrain (petersham) ribbon, and hand stitch them in place.

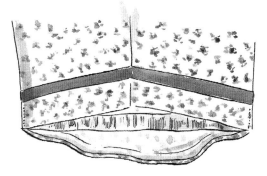

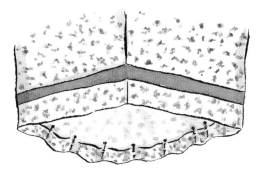

7 Cut a piece of elastic long enough to fit snugly around half the child's waist. Slip one end just inside the front waistband and machine stitch in position. Push the other end of the elastic inside the other side of the front waistband and again machine stitch it in place.

8 Fold the top of the back of the pants over by ¹/₂ in. (1 cm), then fold over again to enclose the elastic. Pin and machine stitch along the bottom edge of the back waistband.

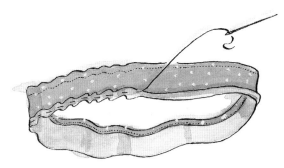

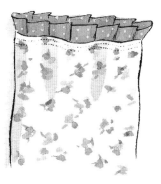

9 Cut two 1¹/₂ x 22-in./4 x 56-cm (1¹/₂ x 22¹/₂-in./4 x 58-cm: 1¹/₂ x 23-in./4 x 60-cm) strips of contrasting fabric for the frills. With right sides together, pin and machine stitch the short ends of each frill together to form a loop, and press the seam open. Turn the bottom edge of each frill to the wrong side by ¹/₄ in. (5 mm) and then again by another ¹/₄ in. (5 mm). Pin and topstitch, stitching as close to the edge as possible. Press.

10 Along the top edge of each frill, press ¹/₄ in. (5 mm) over to the right side. Work a line of running stitch (see page 106) along the top edge, and gather the fabric to fit the bottom of the pants (see pages 106–7). Turn under ³/₈ in. (1 cm) and then another ³/₈ in. (1 cm) to the wrong side at the bottom of the legs, and baste (tack) the hem in place. Pin and baste (tack) the frills around the inside of the legs. Work two rows of machine stitching to hold the frills in place. Press.

Baby bloomers

These cute bloomers are practical as well as stylish. Easy to slip on and off and roomy enough to cover the bulkiest of diapers, they look great with simple T-shirts for everyday wear or with smock tops for a modern take on a classic look. Choose patterned fabrics in crisp cottons for summer or thicker corduroys and denims for winter wear.

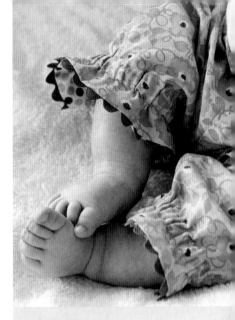

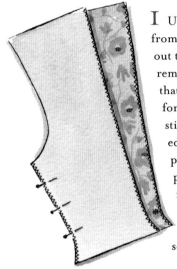

I Using pattern pieces 13 and 38 from the pull-out sheets provided, cut out two front and two back leg pieces, remembering to flip the patterns so that you have a right and a left piece for each leg. Overlock or zigzag stitch along the inner and outer edges and curved edges of each piece. With right sides together, pin and machine stitch the left front and back leg pieces together along the inner edge. Repeat with the right leg pieces. Press the seams open.

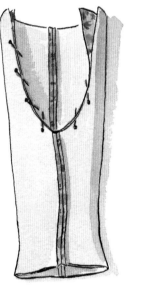

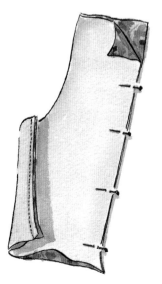

2 With right sides together, pin and machine stitch the right leg pieces together along the outer edges. Repeat with the left leg pieces. Press the seams open.

3 Turn one leg right side out and slip it inside the other leg, so that the right sides are together. Pin together, aligning the inner seams on each leg, and machine stitch along the curved edge. Trim the seam allowance to ¼ in. (5 mm), and overlock or zigzag stitch around it. Turn right side out.

You will need

* *Pattern pieces 13 and 38 from the pull-out section*
* *40 x 28 in. (100 x 70 cm) main fabric*
* *32 x 8 in. (80 x 20 cm) coordinating fabric for lining*
* *18 in. (45 cm) elastic, ⅝ in. (15 mm) wide, for waist*
* *26 in. (65 cm) elastic, ¼ in. (6 mm) wide, for legs*
* *34 in. (85 cm) jumbo rick-rack braid*

SIZES

The patterns are for ages 6–12 months and 12–18 months.

Take ½-in. (1-cm) seam allowances throughout, unless otherwise stated.

4 Cut a 25¹/₄ x 2³/₈-in. (64 x 6-cm) strip of coordinating fabric. Turn under ¹/₂ in. (1 cm) to the wrong side at each short end and press. With right sides together, pin the strip around the top of the bloomers, aligning the folded ends of the strip with the central back seam. Machine stitch in place, ¹/₂ in. (1 cm) from the top edge.

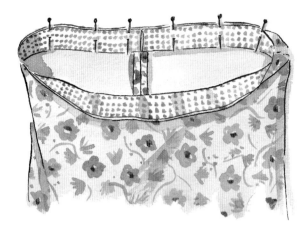

5 Along the raw edge of the strip, turn under ¹/₂ in. (1 cm) to the wrong side and press. Pin and machine stitch in place. Sew another line of stitches just down from the top edge for a neat finish.

6 Cut two lengths of rick-rack braid to fit around the bottom of the legs, adding a little extra for an overlap. Pin and baste (tack) them around the bottom of the legs, aligning the edge of the rick-rack braid with the bottom raw edge of the legs. Overlap the ends slightly.

7 Cut two strips of coordinating fabric 2 in. (5 cm) deep and long enough to fit around the bottom of the legs plus 1 in. (2.5 cm). Press ¹/₂ in. (1 cm) to the wrong side at both short ends of both strips. With right sides together, aligning the raw edges and aligning the folded ends with the inner leg seams, pin the strips around the bottom of the legs. Machine stitch ¹/₂ in. (1 cm) from the edge.

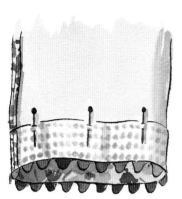

8 Turn the bloomers wrong side out. Press under ½ in. (1 cm) along the top edge of the strip and pin and machine stitch it in place. Make another line of stitching ¾ in. (2 cm) down from this to form a channel through which to thread the elastic.

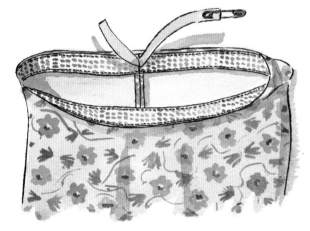

9 Attach a safety pin to the end of the wider elastic and thread it through the waist channel, passing it through the opening. Gather the bloomers. When the waist is the required size, machine stitch the ends of the elastic securely together and push them inside the channel. Slipstitch the opening closed (see page 105).

10 Thread the thinner elastic through the channels at the bottom of the legs in the same way. Gather the legs. When the legs are the required width, machine stitch the ends of the elastic securely together and push them inside the channel. Slipstitch the opening closed.

SKIRTS & DRESSES 4

Corduroy skirt

Corduroy fabric is great for children's clothes as it is so hard-wearing. Here it has been brightened up with a pretty floral border and finished off with beautiful velvet ribbon trim. The skirt is made from the whole width of the fabric, with the length being adjusted to fit the size required.

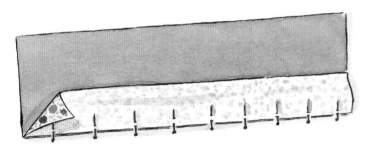

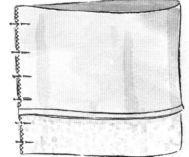

1 Using the full width of the fabrics, cut a rectangle of corduroy fabric 9½ (10¼: 11) in./ 24 (26: 28) cm deep and piece of floral fabric 6 in. (15 cm) deep. With right sides together, pin and machine stitch the floral fabric along the bottom edge of the corduroy fabric. Press the seam toward the floral fabric.

2 Overlock or zigzag stitch along both short sides. With right sides together, fold the panel over and align these edges. Pin and stitch these together to form a tube. Press the seam open. Turn right side out.

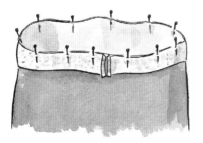

3 Cut a piece of floral fabric 2¼ in. (5.5 cm) deep x the initial width of the corduroy fabric. Fold under ⅜ in. (1 cm) at each short end of this strip to the wrong side, and press. With right sides together, pin and machine stitch the strip to the top of the skirt piece.

You will need

* Template on page 110
* 45 x 14 in. (115 x 35 cm) corduroy fabric
* 45 x 8 in. (115 x 20 cm) floral fabric
* Approx. 20 in. (50 cm) elastic, ¾ in. (2 cm) wide
* Approx. 48 in. (120 cm) velvet ribbon, ⅝ in. (18 mm) wide
* Button, approx. ¾ in. (2 cm) in diameter

SIZES

The patterns are for ages 2–3, 3–4, and 4–5 years.

Take ½-in. (1-cm) seam allowances throughout, unless otherwise stated.

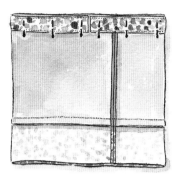

4 Turn the skirt wrong side out. Along the top edge of the floral strip, press ½ in. (1 cm) over to the wrong side. Fold the floral strip over along the seam line, then pin this folded edge onto the corduroy. Machine stitch, stitching as near to the fold as you can, to form a channel, leaving a small opening of about 1 in. (2.5 cm). Topstitch just below the top edge.

5 Using the template on page 110, cut one pocket from corduroy and one from floral fabric. With right sides together, pin and machine stitch the pieces together, leaving a small opening in one side. Snip the seam allowance and turn right side out. Press. Work a line of running stitch (see page 106) across the top to gather the pocket to roughly 2⅜ in. (6 cm) and finish with a few small stitches to hold it in place.

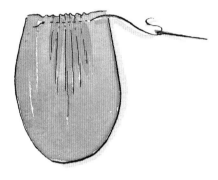

6 Cut a 3 x 1½-in. (8 x 4-cm) rectangle of floral fabric. With right sides together, pin and machine stitch this piece to the top of the pocket piece. Fold in the ends in by ½ in. (1 cm) and fold over to the back of the pocket. Slipstitch in place.

7 Place the pocket on the skirt and pin in place. Topstitch around the pocket, close to the edge. Fold the bottom edge of the skirt under by ½ in. (1 cm) and pin this edge to the wrong side of the skirt, aligning the fold with the stitch line of the floral fabric.

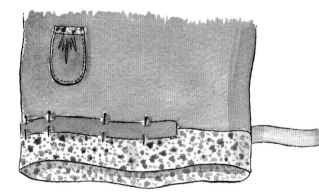

8 Pin and machine stitch the velvet ribbon along the top of the floral border on the skirt, stitching as close to the edges of the ribbon as possible. Overlap the ends of the ribbon slightly and fold them under.

9 Cut one length of elastic to fit around the top with a small overlap. Using a safety pin, feed the elastic through the waistband channel (see page 108). Machine stitch the ends of the elastic together, then slipstitch the opening closed (see page 105).

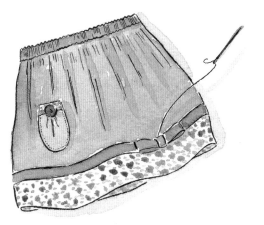

10 Cut a piece of velvet ribbon about 7½ in. (19 cm) long, and form into a loop, securing with a few hand stitches. Wrap a second piece of ribbon about 2¼ in. (5.5 cm) long around the middle of the loop to form the bow, and stitch in place. Hand stitch the bow onto the ribbon border at the front of the skirt. Sew a button onto the pocket.

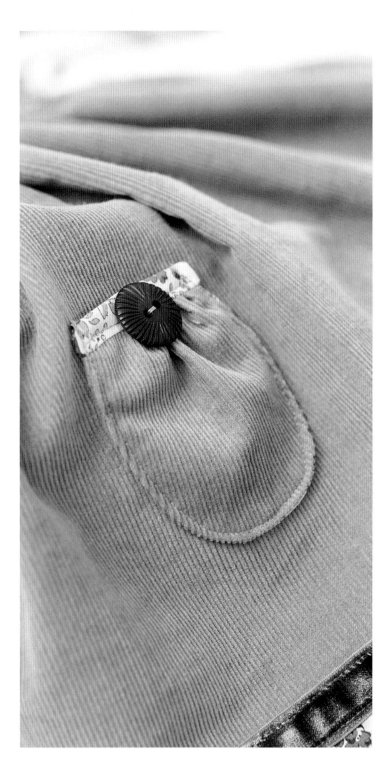

Puffball skirt

This great little skirt is very easy to make and works well for lots of different occasions. Make it from patterned cotton fabric and it is a practical and easy-to-wear everyday skirt; alternatively, use beautiful velvet, with a coordinating lining fabric for the inner skirt—perfect for a party outfit that little girls will love. Avoid very thick fabrics so that the skirt does not become too bulky.

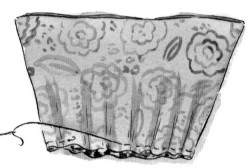

1 Using pattern piece 4 from the pull-out sheets provided, cut out two pieces from the main fabric. With right sides together, pin and machine stitch them together along the two short sides. Press the seams open.

2 Work a line of running stitch around the bottom edge and gather the piece (see pages 106–7). Set this piece to one side, leaving the thread loose for Step 4.

3 Using pattern piece 12 from the pull-out sheet, cut out two lining pieces. With right sides together, pin and machine stitch them together along the side edges. Press the seams open.

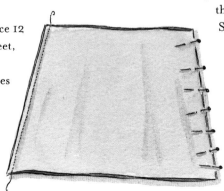

TIPS

Try using really bold colors and patterns for this puffball skirt to give it a bright and contemporary look. To add pockets, follow the instructions for the elasticated skirt and stitch them in place before you gather and sew the waistband in place.

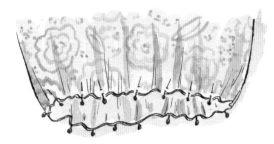

4 With right sides together, put the lining inside the main skirt section. Gather the skirt (see pages 106–7) so that the lining fits snugly inside, ensuring that the seams of both layers align. Make a few stitches at the end of the running stitches to hold them in place. Pin and machine stitch the lining to the main skirt, ensuring that the gathers look even all the way around.

5 Turn the skirt and lining right side out and press the seam flat. Push the lining inside the skirt. Work a line of running stitch around the top of the skirt (but not the lining) and gather it so that the lining sits snugly, again aligning the seams of both layers. Finish off the running stitch with a few small stitches. Pin and baste (tack) the lining to the gathered top of the skirt.

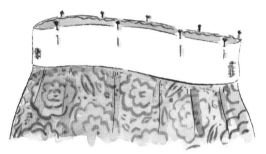

6 Using pattern piece 11 from the pull-out sheets, cut two waistband sections from the lining fabric and two from interfacing. Following the manufacturer's instructions, iron one piece of interfacing to the wrong side of each waistband piece. Machine stitch two buttonholes as indicated on the pattern. Snip them open (see page 108).

7 With right sides together, pin and machine stitch the two waistband pieces together along the short sides to form a loop. Press the seams open. Place the waistband around the top of the skirt, right sides together, with the buttonholes at the bottom and the raw edges aligning. Pin in place, aligning the seams of the waistband with the seams of the skirt and lining, and machine stitch together.

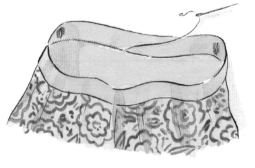

8 Turn under 3/8 in. (1 cm) to the wrong side along the buttonhole edge of the waistband. Pin and slipstitch neatly to the inside of the skirt (see page 105).

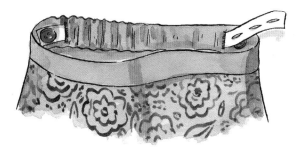

9 Sew a button about ³/₄ in. (2 cm) along from each buttonhole. Using a safety pin, thread a length of buttonhole elastic about 12 in. (30 cm) long through the buttonholes, and fasten one end to one of the buttons. Remove the safety pin, try the skirt on the child to check the sizing, and fasten the other end of the elastic to the other button.

10 Cut a piece of velvet ribbon about 30 in. (75 cm) long and form it into a loop. Make a few stitches in the middle to hold it in place and gather it slightly. Cut another piece about 4 in. (10 cm) long, and stitch it around the center of the loop, with the ends at the back, to form a bow. Cross the ends of a 16-in. (40-cm) length of ribbon over one another, as shown. Pin to the skirt, velvet side up, and sew the bow on top to finish.

Gypsy skirt

This simple sweet-looking gypsy skirt is made from three tiers of slightly gathered fabric, so it's fabulously floaty. Light cotton fabrics work well for a summer skirt or try heavier corduroys and linens for the colder winter months.

I Cut three strips of fabric for the different tiers of the skirt, using the measurements given on the right. (Join two strips together to make a piece the correct length if necessary.) Overlock or zigzag stitch along the bottom edge and the two short sides of the top tier. With right sides together, pin and stitch the two short edges together. Press the seam open. Along the top edge, press under 3/8 in. (1 cm) and then another 3/4 in. (2 cm) to the wrong side. Pin and machine stitch in place, leaving an opening of about 1 1/4 in. (3 cm) for the elastic.

2 Overlock or zigzag stitch around all four sides of the middle tier of fabric. Using a needle and thread, work a line of running stitch all the way around the top edge (see page 106). Pull the thread to gather the strip (see pages 106–7), so that it is the same width as the bottom of the top tier.

3 With right sides together, pin and machine stitch the gathered middle tier to the bottom of the top tier, making sure that the gathers are even all the way around. Baste (tack) in place, and then machine stitch. Repeat Steps 2 and 3 to attach the bottom tier.

4 To hem the bottom of the skirt, turn under 3/8 in. (1 cm) and then another 3/8 in. (1 cm) to the wrong side, pin, and machine stitch in place. Press. Pin and stitch ribbon along the joins of the tiers, folding the ends of the ribbon under for a neat finish. Press. Cut a piece of elastic 18 1/2 in./47 cm (19 1/4 in./49 cm: 20 in./51 cm) long. Feed it through the waistband channel, and secure at both ends (see page 108). Machine stitch the channel opening closed.

You will need

* Fabric A (top tier): 36 1/2 x 5 1/2 in./ 93 x 14 cm (37 1/2 x 6 1/4 in./95 x 16 cm: 38 1/4 x 7 in./97 x 18 cm)

* Fabric B (middle tier): 44 1/2 x 4 1/2 in./113 x 11 cm (45 1/2 x 5 1/4 in./ 115 x 13 cm: 46 1/4 x 6 in./117 x 15 cm)

* Fabric C (bottom tier): 52 1/2 x 4 3/4 in. /133 x 12 cm (53 1/4 x 5 1/2 in./ 135 x 14 cm; 54 x 6 1/4 in./137 x 16 cm) Join 2 strips together to make the length if necessary.

* 83 in. (210 cm) ribbon, 3/8 in. (9 mm) wide

* 20 in. (51 cm) elastic, 5/8 in. (15 mm) wide

SIZES

The patterns are for ages 2–3, 3–4, and 4–5 years.

Take 1/2-in. (1-cm) seam allowances throughout, unless otherwise stated.

Pinafore dress

The classic cut of this pinafore dress will fit and flatter all shapes and sizes. Lining the dress gives it a smart, crisp finish that makes it suitable for an everyday dress as well as a special-occasion outfit. Flower decorations made from fabric yo-yos add a modern twist to the traditional look and are very easy to make, using scraps of fabrics in colors that coordinate with the dress. Stitch the yo-yos firmly in place, so that they will withstand washing and wear and tear.

You will need

* Pattern pieces 21 and 26 from the pull-out section and template on page 111

* 53 x 28 in. (134 x 72 cm) main fabric

* 53 x 28 in. (134 x 72 cm) lining fabric

* Scraps of fabric for flowers and leaves

* Approx. 18 in. (45 cm) ribbon, 1/4 in. (6 mm) wide, for stalks

* Approx. 8 x 3 1/4 in. (20 x 8 cm) fusible bonding web

* 3 buttons, 3/4 in. (2 cm) in diameter, for flowers

* 4 buttons, 3/4 in. (2 cm) in diameter, for back

SIZES

The patterns are for ages 2–3, 3–4, and 4–5 years.

Take 1/2-in. (1-cm) seam allowances throughout, unless otherwise stated.

I Using pattern pieces 21 and 26 from the pull-out sheets provided, cut one front and two back pieces from both the main and the lining fabrics, making sure there is one left and one right back piece in each fabric. With right sides together, pin and machine stitch the main fabric back pieces to the front piece at the shoulders. Press the seams open. Repeat, using the lining fabric pieces.

2 With right sides together (if applicable), pin and machine stitch the lining piece to the main fabric piece around the neck and armholes, aligning the shoulder seams. Trim the seam allowances to 1/4 in. (5 mm). Turn right side out by pulling the back sections through the shoulder straps. Press so that all the seams lie flat.

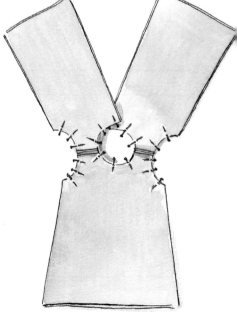

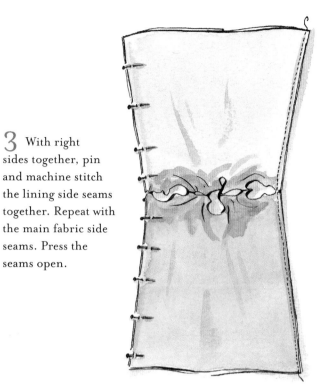

3 With right sides together, pin and machine stitch the lining side seams together. Repeat with the main fabric side seams. Press the seams open.

4 Cut lengths of ribbon $7^{1}/_{2}$, $5^{1}/_{2}$, and $4^{1}/_{2}$ in. (19, 14, and 11 cm) long. Pin and machine stitch them onto the front of the dress, as indicated on the pattern, to form the flower stalks. Sew along both sides of the ribbons, stitching as close to the edge as you can. Following the instructions on page 69, make three yo-yos from circles of fabric $4^{3}/_{8}$ in. (11 cm) in diameter. Hand stitch them securely to the front of the dress at the top of the ribbon stalks, making sure that they are firmly attached. Sew a button to the center of each yo-yo.

5 Following the manufacturer's instructions, iron fusible bonding web onto the back of the leaf fabric. Using the template on page 111, cut out four leaf shapes and fuse them onto the dress at the sides of the stalks. Machine stitch around the edge of each leaf.

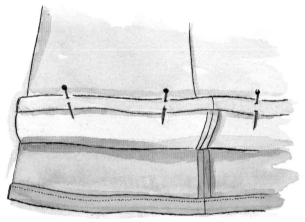

6 Along the bottom edge of the main dress, press under $3/8$ in. (1 cm) and then another $3/8$ in. (1 cm) to the wrong side. Pin and stitch in place to hem the bottom edge. Press. Along the bottom edge of the lining, turn $5/8$ in. (1.5 cm) and then another $5/8$ in. (1.5 cm) under to the wrong side. Pin and stitch in place. Press.

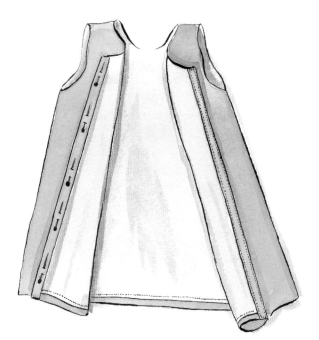

7 To finish the back of the dress, turn over ³/₈ in. (I cm) and then another ³/₄ in. (2 cm) to the wrong side along each center back. Pin and topstitch along both edges and across the top and the bottom of the turnback.

8 Mark the positions of the buttonholes, spacing them 4³/₄ in. (I2 cm) apart (see page I08). Stitch the buttonholes and snip them open. Sew buttons onto the other side of the back to correspond. Press.

Toddler's dress

The beauty of this little dress is all in the detail. Very easy to make, and requiring only a small amount of fabric, it can be stitched in a matter of hours. A pretty yo-yo rosette adds the finishing touch, with a ribbon trim stitched around the bottom for extra decoration. Make rosettes into brooches by sewing a safety pin or a brooch pin to the back, so that they can be worn with lots of different outfits.

I Using pattern pieces 22 and 29 from the pull-out sheets provided, cut one front and one back piece from the main fabric. Overlock or zigzag stitch along the straight sides. With right sides together, pin and machine stitch the back and front together along the sides. Press the seams open.

2 Using the lines on the pattern pieces, cut out one front lining and one back lining piece from the dress fabric. (Alternatively, use a coordinating fabric for a decorative detail.) With right sides together, pin and machine stitch them together along the sides. Turn under 3/8 in. (1 cm) and then another 3/8 in. (1 cm) around the bottom, and stitch in place to hem. Press.

3 Turn the main dress right side out. Slip the lining over it, so that the right sides are together. Pin and machine stitch the main dress and lining together around the armholes. Make small snips in the seams (see page 106) and turn right side out. Press.

You will need

* Pattern pieces 22 and 29 from the pull-out section

* 40 in. (100 cm) square of fabric

* 47 in. (120 cm) each of two thin ribbons, 3/8 in. (1 cm) wide

* Scraps of two fabrics, at least 8 in. (20 cm) square, for rosette

* Button, approx. 3/4 in. (2 cm) in diameter

SIZE

The dress is 14 1/4 in. (36 cm) wide by whatever length is required.

Take 1/2-in. (1-cm) seam allowances throughout, unless otherwise stated.

4 Along the front and back top edges, turn under 3/8 in. (1 cm) and then another 5/8 in. (1.5 cm) to the inside. Pin and stitch in place, stitching close to the first folded edge, to form a channel.

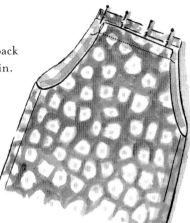

5 Turn the dress wrong side out. Check the length on the child and cut off any excess fabric if necessary. To hem, turn 3/8 in. (1 cm) and then another 3/4 in. (2 cm) to the wrong side. Pin and stitch in place. Press.

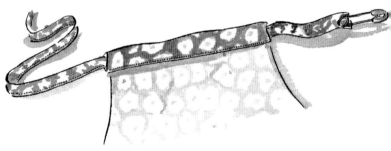

6 Pin and machine stitch two rows of ribbon around the bottom of the dress, positioning the first one along the hem stitching line and the second just above the first. Overlap the ends slightly and turn the ends under for a neat finish.

7 Cut two 1 1/2 x 27 1/2-in. (4 x 70-cm) pieces of the dress fabric. Fold both in half along their length and press. Open out again, and fold in the short ends. Fold both raw edges into the middle crease line, press, then fold in half again. Machine stitch along the length to make the drawstring cords. Press.

8 Using a safety pin, thread one cord through the channel at the top of the front of the dress and one through the channel at the back of the dress. When tied in bows, these cords form the shoulder straps.

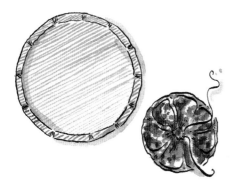

9 Using a compass, draw a circle 5⅛ in. (13 cm) in diameter on scrap paper. Cut out and use as a pattern piece to cut a circle of fabric. Make another circle of fabric in the same way, 3⅛ in. (8 cm) in diameter. Press under ¼ in. (5 mm) all the way around to the wrong side. Work a line of running stitch (see page 106) all the way around the edge of each circle, and pull the thread to gather to form two yo-yos. Finish with a few small stitches. Press.

10 Sew the two yo-yos together, with a button in the center. Fold two lengths of ribbon in half and hold them at the back of the rosette. Hand stitch the rosette onto the front of the dress, stitching through the middle of the lengths of ribbon.

Party dress

This party dress is perfect for special occasions—little girls will love it! The simple bodice is enhanced with sequins and a pretty flower decoration, and the full skirt makes it ideal for dancing around. Shimmering silk has been used here, but a printed cotton fabric would work just as well to make a pretty summer dress.

You will need

* Pattern pieces 33 and 35 from the pull-out section and template on page 110

* 45 x 44 in. (114 x 110 cm) main fabric

* 12 x 40 in. (30 x 100 cm) lining fabric

* 32 in. (82 cm) string sequins

* 9 in. (23 cm) square each of 2 coordinating fabrics for flower

* 7 buttons, 5/8 in. (15 mm) in diameter

SIZES

The patterns are for ages 2–3, 3–4, and 4–5 years.

Take 1/2-in. (1-cm) seam allowances throughout, unless otherwise stated.

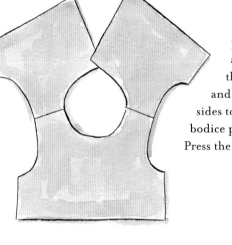

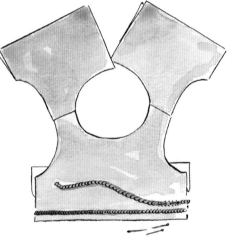

I Using pattern pieces 33 and 35 from the pull-out sheets provided, cut out one front bodice and two back bodice pieces from both the main and the lining fabric, making sure that there is one left and one right bodice piece in each fabric. With right sides together, pin and machine stitch the main fabric back bodice pieces to the front bodice piece at the shoulders. Press the seams open. Repeat, using the lining fabric pieces.

2 With right sides together, pin and machine stitch the lining to the main fabric piece around the armholes and the neck, aligning the shoulder seams. Trim the seam allowances to 1/4 in. (5 mm) and turn right side out. Press neatly, so that the lining does not show from the front.

3 Cut two 16-in. (40-cm) lengths of sequins. Pin one across the front of the bodice, 3/4 in. (2 cm) from the bottom edge, and the second one about 5/8 in. (1.5 cm) above it. Make sure that the sequins are pinned only to the main fabric, and not to the lining. Machine stitch the sequins in place, sewing directly along the middle of the sequins. Trim the ends neatly.

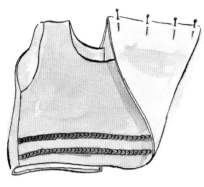

4 With right sides together, pin and machine stitch the bodice pieces together along the side seams and back edges. Repeat with the lining bodice sides. Press the seams open.

5 For the skirt, cut one 16½ x 34-in./42 x 88-cm (18 x 35½-in./46 x 88-cm: 20 x 37½-in./53 x 96-cm) piece for the front, and two 16½ x 18½-in./ 42 x 47-cm (18 x 19½-in. /46 x 50-cm: 20½ x 21½-in./53 x 55-cm) pieces for the backs. Overlock or zigzag stitch along the outer edge of each piece. With right sides together, pin and machine stitch the back pieces to the front along the side seams, making sure that the outer edges align exactly. Press the seams open.

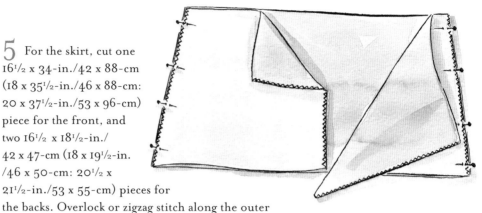

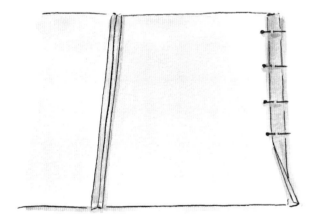

6 Along both center back edges of the skirt, turn over ³⁄8 in. (I cm) and then another I½ in. (4 cm) to the wrong side. Pin and topstitch close to the first fold line on both pieces to form a placket. Press.

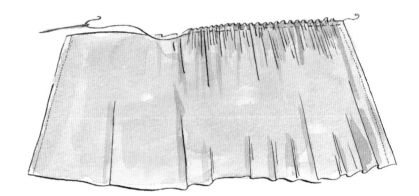

7 Using a needle and thread, work a line of running stitch along the top edge of the skirt (see page 106). Starting from the vertical stitch line on the back of the skirt, so that the placket remains flat, gather the skirt (see pages 106–7). Gather one back piece to a width of 7 in./18 cm (7¼ in./18.5 cm: 7½ in./19 cm), including the placket, and make a few stitches at the side seam to hold the thread in position. Then gather the front section to 12¾ in./32 cm (13 in./33 cm: 13¼ in./34 cm), again making a few stitches at the side seam. Finally, gather the other back section to 7 in./18 cm (7¼ in./18.5 cm: 7½ in./19 cm), including the placket, as before.

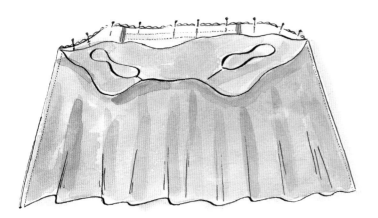

8 With right sides together, aligning the raw edges, lay the skirt along the bottom edge of the front of the bodice. Pin and baste (tack) in position, making sure that the gathers are even. Machine stitch in place. Press the seam toward the top.

9 Along the bottom edge of the inside of the bodice, press under 3/8 in. (1 cm) to the wrong side. Pin and hand stitch in place, aligning the folded edge with the stitch line so that no stitches will show on the front of the dress.

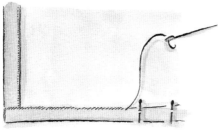

10 To hem the bottom of the dress, turn under 3/8 in. (1 cm) and then another 5/8 in. (1.5 cm) along the bottom edge. Either hand stitch or machine stitch in place. Press the whole dress.

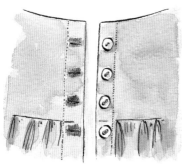

11 Mark the positions of the buttonholes. Stitch the buttonholes and snip them open (see page 108). Sew the buttons onto the other placket to correspond.

FOR THE FLOWER DECORATION
Using the template on page 110, follow the steps for the hairband flower on page 103, making the center flower the same size as the outer flower and omitting the button. For fabric that is prone to fraying, iron fusible bonding web onto the back of the fabric before you cut out the flowers.

Pajamas

These kimono-style pajamas are designed to be unisex—perfect nightwear for boys and girls alike. Don't let the fact that this is one of the more time-consuming projects in this book put you off, as they are easy to make and definitely worth the time and effort. Choose soft cotton fabrics, using brushed cottons for cosy winter pjs, and more lightweight cloth for summer ones.

You will need

* Pattern pieces 14, 16, 18, and 39 from the pull-out section

* 79 x 40 in. (200 x 100 cm) main fabric for pajama top

* 45 x 30 in. (115 x 75 cm) for pajama bottoms

* 45 x 12 in. (115 x 75 cm) edging fabric

* Approx. 22 in. (55 cm) elastic, ³/₄ in. (18 mm) wide

* Approx. 2 in. (5 cm) ribbon ¹/₈ in. (3 mm) wide

* Button, approx. ¹/₂ in. (12 mm) wide

SIZES

The patterns are for ages 2–3, 3–4, and 4–5 years.

Take ¹/₂-in. (1-cm) seam allowances throughout, unless otherwise stated.

PAJAMA TOP

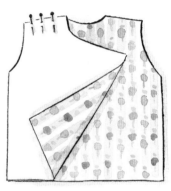

I Using pattern pieces 14, 18, and 39 from the pull-out sheets provided, cut out one back piece, two front pieces, and two sleeves from the main fabric. Overlock or zigzag stitch along the side edges of the back, fronts, and sleeves, and the curved side of the sleeve head. With right sides together, pin and machine stitch the front pieces to the back at the shoulders. Press the seams open.

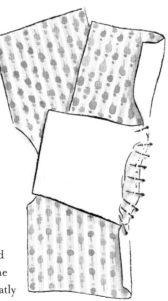

2 With right sides together, pin and machine stitch one of the sleeves to the main body piece, easing the fabric neatly around the curve. Press the seam open.

3 Attach the other sleeve to the other side of the main body piece in the same way. Press the seam open.

THEN the mouse came out
of her jam pot, and Ben-
took the paper bag off
head, and they told the
tale.

...amin and Flopsy were
...pair, they could not
...the string.

Mrs. Tittlemouse was
...ourceful person. She
...ed a hole in the bottom
...er of the sack.

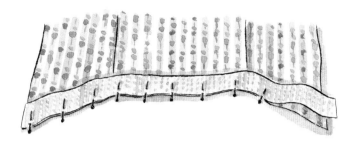

4 With right sides together, fold the sleeves in half. Pin and machine stitch along the underarm seams and down the sides of the body. Press the seams open.

5 Cut a piece of edging fabric long enough to fit along the bottom edge of the pajama top and 3¼ in. (8 cm) deep. With right sides together, aligning the raw edges, pin and machine stitch the strip along the bottom edge of the pajama top. Press the seam toward the bottom edge.

6 Turn the top over and press under ⅜ in. (1 cm) to the wrong side along the length of the edging fabric. Pin and slipstitch (see page 105) the edging in place, making sure that the original stitch line is covered. Press.

7 Cut two pieces of edging fabric on the bias that are long enough to fit along the fronts and 1½ in. (4 cm) deep (see page 107). Fold under ⅜ in. (1 cm) to the wrong side at one short end of both pieces. With the right side of the strip on the wrong side of the fronts and the folded ends at the bottom edge, pin and machine stitch one strip along each raw edge of the two front sections. Press the seams toward the edging strip.

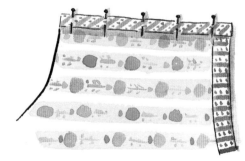

8 Turn the top over. Along both edging strips, press ⅜ in. (1 cm) to the wrong side. Pin and topstitch to the front of the top.

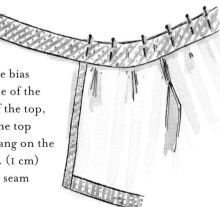

9 Cut a piece of edging fabric measuring 37½ x 1½ in. (95 x 4 cm) on the bias (see page 107). With the right side of the edging strip on the wrong side of the top, pin and machine stitch it along the top edge of the top, leaving an overhang on the left-hand side and turning ⅜ in. (1 cm) under at the other end. Press the seam toward the edging strip.

IO Turn the top over. Along the length of the edging strip, press under $^3/_8$ in. (I cm) to the wrong side. Pin and topstitch it onto the front of the top, forming the overhang into a tie. Press.

II To make the other tie, cut a $8^3/_4$ x $I^1/_2$-in. (22 x 4-cm) piece of edging fabric on the bias. Fold it in half along the length and press. Fold in $^3/_8$ in. (I cm) at each short end. Fold the long edges in to the middle crease on the wrong side, press, fold in half again, pin, and machine stitch, stitching as close to the edge as possible. Stitch one end onto the front of the top in the correct position, so that the ties can form a bow.

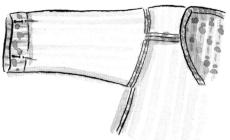

I2 With the top inside out, turn under $^3/_8$ in. (I cm) and then another $^3/_4$ in. (2 cm) on both arms to form the cuffs. Machine stitch in place. Turn the top right side out.

I3 To fasten the top, stitch a small ribbon loop to the top of the inside front and a small button to the inside seam.

PAJAMA BOTTOMS

I Using pattern piece 16 from the pull-out sheets provided, cut two legs from the main fabric. Overlock or zigzag stitch from the top to the bottom of both pieces. With right sides together, fold each leg in half. Pin and machine stitch along the inner seams. Press the seams open.

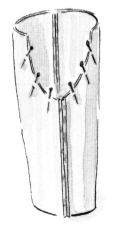

2 With right sides together, slip one leg over the other, aligning the inner leg seams. Pin and stitch around the crotch to join the legs together.

3 With the pajama bottoms wrong side out, press 3/8 in. (1 cm) over to the wrong side along the top edge. Fold this edge over by another 5/8 in. (1.5 cm) pin, and stitch in place, leaving a small opening for the elastic. Press.

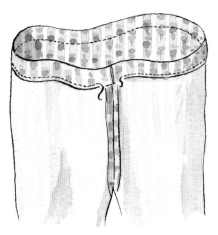

4 Cut two pieces of edging fabric long enough to go around the bottom of the legs and 1½ in. (4 cm) deep on the bias (see page 107). Fold each one in half widthwise, right sides together, and stitch the short edges together. Press the seams open. Slip the edging wrong side out over the bottom of the legs. Pin and stitch them together, aligning the seams. Press the seams toward the edging.

5 Turn the pajama bottoms right side out. Turn under 3/8 in. (1 cm) to the wrong side along the raw edge of the edging strips. Pin and topstitch this folded edge onto the right side of the bottoms, stitching as close to the fold as possible.

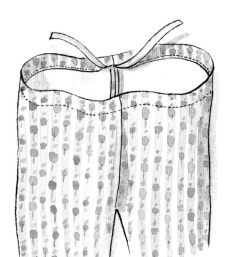

6 Thread the elastic through the waist channel, secure the elastic, and machine stitch the opening closed (see page 108). Press.

Dressing gown

Make this project in a favorite printed fabric and line with a soft brushed cotton for a truly cute and snuggly dressing gown that your little ones are sure to love. If you want to include patch pockets, follow the instructions for the simple shirt on page 35, and stitch them onto the front of the gown before you attach the lining.

1 Using pattern pieces 23, 27, and 37 from the pull-out sheets provided, cut out one back, two fronts, and two sleeves from the main fabric, making sure that you cut one right and one left front. With right sides together, pin and machine stitch the fronts to the back at the shoulders. Press the seams open.

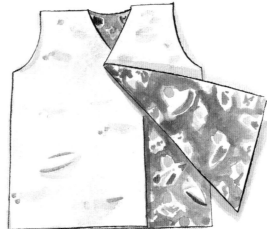

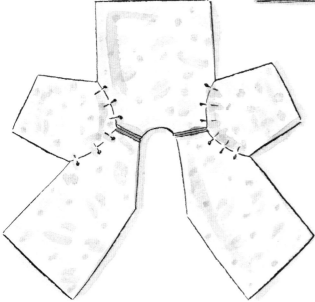

2 With right sides together, pin the sleeves around the curve of the armholes. Machine stitch, snip the curved seams, then press the seams open.

You will need

* *Pattern pieces 23, 27, and 37 from the pull-out section*

* *79 x 45 in. (200 x 115 cm) main fabric*

* *79 x 45 in. (200 x 115 cm) brushed cotton fabric for lining*

SIZES

The patterns are for ages 2–3, 3–4, and 4–5 years.

Take ½-in. (1-cm) seam allowances throughout, unless otherwise stated.

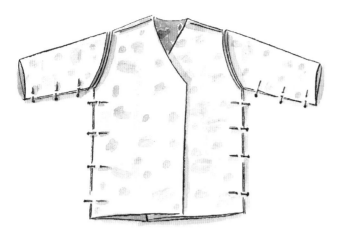

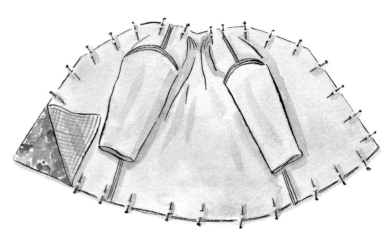

3 Pin and machine stitch the underarm and side seams, then press the seams open. Repeat Steps 1 through 3, using the lining fabric.

4 With right sides together, slip the lining over the gown. Starting at the neck and aligning the outer edges and the seams, pin the main gown and lining together down the sides and along the bottom edge, and machine stitch, leaving an opening of about 6 in. (15 cm) along the bottom edge. Snip the corners off (see page 106) and make small snips around the curved front seam allowances so that the fronts will lie flat.

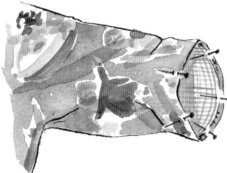

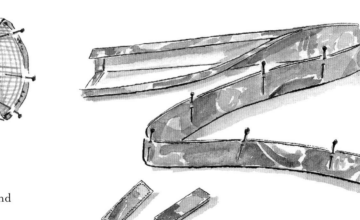

5 Turn right side out and press. Hand stitch the opening in the bottom edge closed. Turn the outer cuff to the wrong side by ³⁄₈ in. (1 cm) and the lining cuff to its wrong side by the same amount. Pin and topstitch around both cuffs and press. Topstitch all the way around the edge of the gown about ³⁄₈ in. (1 cm) from the edge.

6 Cut a 44 x 3¹⁄₄-in. (112 x 8-cm) strip of the main fabric for the tie. Press ³⁄₈ in. (1 cm) to the wrong side all the way around. Fold the strip in half and press. Pin and topstitch all the way round to form the belt. Cut two 2³⁄₄ x 1¹⁄₂-in. (7 x 4-cm) strips for the belt loops. Press ³⁄₈ in. (1 cm) to the wrong side all the way around on both pieces. Fold both pieces in half, and topstitch all the way around. Pin and stitch the loops onto the side seams about 9 in. (23 cm) from the bottom, and thread the belt through.

Nightdress

This nightdress is made from just two pattern pieces, in the same way as the petal top on page 20, leaving the sleeves ungathered. Use lightweight cotton for the warmer months or soft brushed cotton for a cozy finish that will give sweet dreams all night long. A simple ribbon bow adds the finishing touch.

You will need

* Pattern pieces 3 and 17 from the pull-out section

* 52 x 40 in. (130 x 100 cm) main fabric

* Approx. 18 in. (45 cm) elastic, ¼ in. (6 mm) wide

* Approx. 36 in. (90 cm) ribbon, ½ in. (12 mm) wide

SIZES

The patterns are for ages 2—3, 3—4, and 4—5 years.

Take ½-in. (1-cm) seam allowances throughout, unless otherwise stated.

I Using pattern pieces 3 and 17 from the pull-out sheets provided, cut out two body pieces and two sleeves. Overlock or zigzag stitch along the sides and the shoulder seams. With right sides together, pin and machine stitch one curve of each sleeve to one of the body pieces. Press the seams open.

2 Pin and machine stitch the other curve of each sleeve to the other body piece, as in Step I. Press the seams open.

3 With right sides together, pin and machine stitch the sides of the body and both underarm seams. Press the seams open.

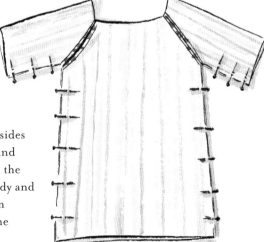

TIP
The pattern for this sweet
little nightdress will really
come in handy. Quick and
easy to sew, it can be used
and adapted to make the
perfect shepherd, angel, or
fairy outfit—ideal for school
plays and dressing-up parties.

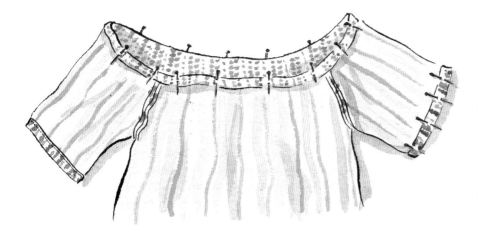

4 Around the neck, turn under 3/8 in. (1 cm) and then another 3/8 in. (1 cm) to the wrong side. Pin and machine stitch, stitching as close to the fold line as possible, leaving an opening of about 1 1/4 in. (3 cm) for the elastic. Do not worry too much about any puckers in the fabric around the curves, as these will not show when the neck is gathered. Repeat on the sleeves, without leaving an opening.

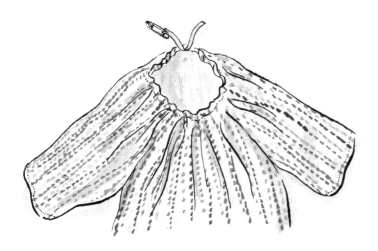

5 Using a safety pin, feed the elastic through the channel in the neck (see page 108). Machine stitch the ends of the elastic together, push the elastic into the channel, and machine stitch the opening closed.

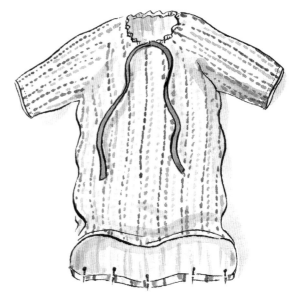

6 Machine stitch the middle of the ribbon onto the top front of the nightdress, then tie it in a neat bow. Trim the ends neatly. Check the length of the nightdress on the child, and trim off any excess fabric if necessary. Turn under 3/8 in. (1 cm) and then another 5/8 in. (1.5 cm) to the wrong side around the base of the nightdress. Pin and machine stitch in place, stitching as close to the fold as possible. Press.

NIGHTDRESS

ACCESSORIES 6

Apron

Children love doing messy things like painting and baking, and this apron is the perfect cover-up to keep their clothes clean. Made from cotton fabric, it is easily washable and has a large pocket to keep things close at hand. For a waterproof version, cut the apron from oilcloth fabric, omitting the backing fabric, and edge with bias binding; stitch a length of ribbon across the back to form the ties.

I Cut two 12½ x 31-in. (31 x 81-cm) rectangles of fabric—one from the front fabric and one from the backing fabric. Cut a head hole 8¼ in. (21 cm) from the top of each piece; the hole should be centered on the width of the fabric and 5½ in. deep x 5 in. wide (14 cm deep x 12.5 cm wide).

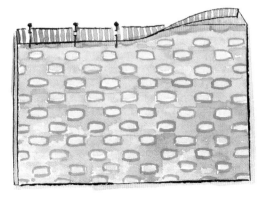

2 Cut a 12¼ x 15½-in. (31 x 39-cm) piece of fabric for the pocket. Fold it in half, wrong sides together, aligning the short sides. Cut a 12¼ x 2½-in. (31 x 6-cm) piece of binding fabric. With right sides together, pin and machine stitch this strip along the fold of the pocket piece, stitching 1¼ in. (3 cm) from the fold.

You will need

* 52 x 16 in. (132 x 40 cm) fabric for the front and tie
* 12½ x 32 in. (31 x 81 cm) fabric for the backing
* 7½ x 12½ in. (19 x 31 cm) fabric for the pocket
* 3¼ x 24½ in. (8 x 62 cm) fabric for binding

SIZE

One size only, up to age 5.

Take ½-in. (1-cm) seam allowances throughout, unless otherwise stated.

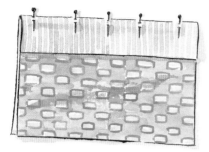

3 Turn the pocket over and press under 3/8 in. (1 cm) along the raw edge of the binding to the wrong side. Pin and machine stitch this edge to the pocket piece. Press.

4 Lay the pocket right side up on the right side of the front of the apron, then pin and baste (tack) it in place around the three outer edges. With right sides together, pin and stitch the front and backing rectangles together around all four outer sides. Trim the corners and turn right side out, through the gap left for the head. Press.

5 Using pins or a fabric marker pen, mark two stitch lines vertically on the pocket. Machine stitch along these lines, making a few forward and reverse stitches at the top for extra strength.

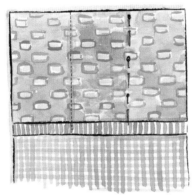

6 Cut a 52 x 3¹/₄-in. (132 x 8-cm) strip of the fabric used for the back of the apron. Fold it in half widthwise, with right sides together. Pin, then machine stitch along one short side and the long side. Snip off the corners at the stitched end and turn right side out. Press and turn in the open end and slipstitch closed (see page 105).

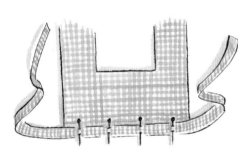

7 Lay the strip centrally across the bottom of the right side of the back of the apron, and pin in place. Machine stitch.

8 Cut a 1¹/₂ x 24¹/₂-in. (4 x 62-cm) strip of binding fabric. Fold one short end over to the wrong side by 3/8 in. (1 cm), and press. With right sides together, pin and machine stitch this strip around the head hole, stitching 3/8 in. (1 cm) from the edge of the hole. Overlap the ends slightly, and fold the binding at the corners. Press 3/8 in. (1 cm) under along the raw edge of the binding. Pin and slipstitch this edge to the back of the apron, making sure that the corners look neat. Press.

Double-sided hat

Let your little ones have fun in the sun with this sweet summer hat. Use two contrasting fabrics to make it reversible, choosing light- to mediumweight cottons and adding interfacing to help the hat keep its shape. You could also use a waterproof fabric for a showerproof hat, making it perfect for wet weather, too.

You will need

* Pattern pieces 9 and 10 from the pull-out section

* 20 x 40 in. (50 x 100 cm) fabric A (light- or mediumweight cotton, denim, corduroy, or linen)

* 20 x 40 in. (50 x 100 cm) fabric B, (similar weight as fabric A)

* 16 in. (40 cm) square of mediumweight iron-on interfacing

SIZES

The patterns are for ages 1–3 and 3–5 years.

Take ½-in. (1-cm) seam allowances throughout, unless otherwise stated.

I From fabric A, cut six of pattern piece 10 from the pull-out sheets provided. With right sides together, pin and machine stitch two pieces together along one side. Press the seam open. Pin and stitch a third piece to the other side and press the seam open. Repeat, using the remaining three pieces.

2 Cut a 2 x 3-in. (5 x 7-cm) piece of fabric from fabric A. Fold it in half along its length and machine stitch along the long raw edge ½ in. (1 cm) from the edge. Trim the seam allowance and turn the tube right side out. Press. Fold in half to make a small loop. With right sides together, pin and machine stitch the two sections from Step 1 together to form the top of the hat, inserting the fabric loop between the layers, with the raw ends sticking out of the seam. Press the seam open.

3 Using pattern piece 9 from the pull-out sheets, cut out two rim pieces from fabric A and two pieces from iron-on interfacing. Following the manufacturer's instructions, iron the interfacing to the wrong side of the fabric rim pieces. With right sides together, pin and machine stitch the short, straight edges together to form a ring. Press the seams open.

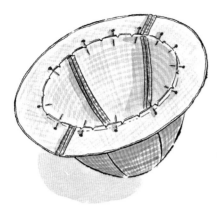

4 With right sides together, pin and machine stitch the rim section to the top of the hat. Make small snips in the seam all the way around for a neat finish.

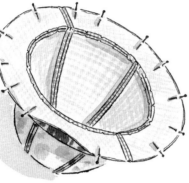

5 Using fabric B, repeat Steps 1 through 4 to make the reversible side of the hat. With right sides together, pin and machine stitch the inner and outer hat pieces together around the rim, leaving an opening of about 2 in. (5 cm). Make small snips all the way around the seam allowance.

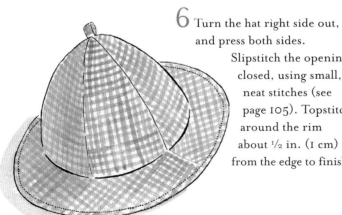

6 Turn the hat right side out, and press both sides. Slipstitch the opening closed, using small, neat stitches (see page 105). Topstitch around the rim about ½ in. (1 cm) from the edge to finish.

Scarf

Appliqué is such an effective way to decorate plain items and this simple spotty design is the perfect starting point for the novice stitcher. Choose the softest wool fabric that you can find (most children won't have anything remotely itchy anywhere near them!) and appliqué spots using scraps of coordinating fabrics. The button detail helps to keep the scarf in place as well as adding a decorative finishing touch.

I Cut the wool fabric and backing fabric to size. Set the backing strip to one side.

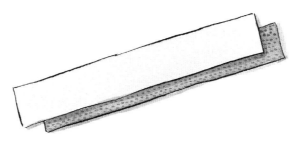

2 Following the manufacturer's instructions, iron fusible bonding web to the back of the scraps of fabric. Using a compass, draw about 16 circles on the backing papers, making some just over 2 in. (5.5 cm) in diameter and some 1½ in. (4 cm) in diameter. Cut out the circles.

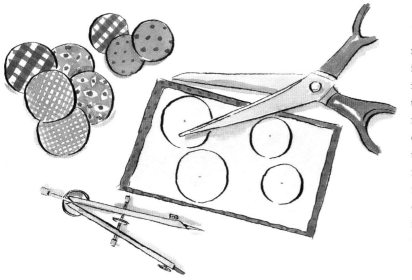

You will need

* *45 x 6½ in. (114 x 16 cm) lightweight wool fabric*

* *45 x 6½ in. (114 x 16 cm) cotton fabric for backing*

* *Selection of coordinating scraps of fabric*

* *Fusible bonding web*

* *Self-covering button, 1½ in. (4 cm) in diameter*

SIZE

Finished scarf measures 44 x 5½ in. (112 x 14 cm).

Take ½-in. (1-cm) seam allowances throughout, unless otherwise stated.

4 Machine stitch around the edges of all of the circles, keeping the stitching as close to the edges as you can. Trim the ends of thread.

3 Arrange the fabric circles on the short ends of the right side of the wool strip from Step I. When you are happy with the arrangement, peel off the backing papers, lay a damp cloth over the wool fabric and circles, and press down for a few seconds with a medium-hot iron to fuse the circles in place.

5 With right sides together, pin and stitch the scarf to the backing fabric and machine stitch, leaving an opening of about 4 in. (IO cm) along one side. Turn the scarf right side out, push the corners out neatly, and press. Slipstitch the opening closed (see page IO5), and topstitch all the way round the scarf.

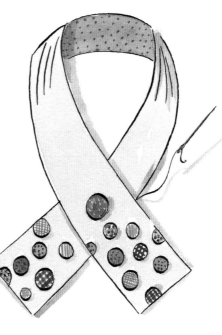

6 Cover the button with a scrap of fabric (see page IO8). Position the button on the scarf, crossing the ends of the scarf over themselves and making sure that the scarf can slip easily over the child's head. Stitch the button in place, stitching through all layers.

POCKET SCARF

A pocket in the scarf is ideal for keeping a little toy close at hand.

Follow Steps 1, 5, and 6, above. Using the template on page 111, cut one pocket shape from the wool fabric and one from the backing fabric. Pin rick-rack braid around the curve of the wool pocket piece. With right sides together, pin and machine stitch the wool piece to the backing pocket piece, leaving a small opening along the straight edge. Turn the pocket right side out and slipstitch the opening closed. Topstitch along the top of the pocket and then machine stitch it onto the scarf.

Poncho

No need to wrestle your child into their coat sleeves with this adorable poncho, which is sure to keep them warm as toast! Choose mediumweight wool fabric, so that it hangs nicely and is not too bulky. A flower brooch makes the perfect finishing touch. This pattern can also be used to make a dressing-up cape that any budding superhero would be delighted to wear.

You will need

* Pattern pieces 31 and 40 from the pull-out section
* 40 in. (100 cm) square of wool fabric
* 40 in. (100 cm) square of lining fabric
* Approx. 70 in. (175 cm) each of two colors of rick-rack braid
* 1 large snap fastener
* Button, 1 in. (2.5 cm) in diameter

SIZES

The patterns are for ages 2–3, 3–4, and 4–5 years.

Take ½-in. (1-cm) seam allowances throughout, unless otherwise stated.

I Using pattern pieces 31 and 40 from the pull-out sheets provided, cut out one back and two front pieces from the wool fabric, making sure that there is a left and a right front. With right sides together, pin and machine stitch the fronts to the back along the outer edges. Press the seams open. Repeat with the lining fabric.

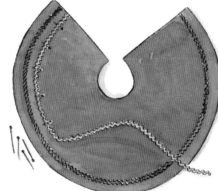

2 Lay the wool fabric poncho right side up on your work surface and smooth it out so that it is flat. Pin and baste (tack) one line of rick-rack braid about 2 in. (5 cm) from the bottom edge, and a second line about ¾ in. (2 cm) above this. Machine stitch the rick-rack in place and trim the ends neatly.

3 Lay the wool fabric poncho right side up on your work surface, with the lining right side down on top, aligning the seams and the outer edges. Make sure it is completely flat. Pin and baste (tack) the two layers together all the way around. Machine stitch, starting on the neck and leaving a 4-in. (10-cm) opening along one side.

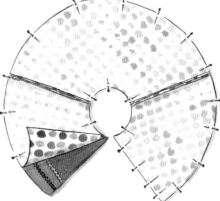

4 Snip off the corners
and turn right side out.
Hand stitch the opening
closed. Press the poncho.
Topstitch all around the
outer edge, about 3/8 in.
(1 cm) from the edge. Stitch
the two sides of a snap
fastener to the top of the
poncho, with a decorative
button on top.

FLOWER BROOCH

To make the flower brooch,
use the large flower template
on page 110 and cut out three
flower shapes from three
shades of felt. Stitch them
together in the center, and
sew a button in the middle.
Stitch a brooch pin (which
you can buy from any good
haberdashery store) or a
safety pin to the back.

Hairband

This really is the easiest project to make and is the perfect way to use up fabric scraps. Use fabrics that coordinate with an outfit—for a bridesmaid, for example, or in school colors to match a uniform, Try making them to sell at school fund-raisers: they are sure to be popular and will cost next to nothing to make.

You will need

FOR THE BASIC HAIRBAND

* *16½ x 8 in. (41 x 20 cm) of fabric*
* *6 in. (15 cm) elastic, ½ in. (12 mm) wide*

FOR THE DECORATIONS

* *Template on page 110*
* *Fabric scraps*
* *Self-covering button (for flower and button decorations)*

SIZE

The finished hairband measures approx. 20½ x 2¼ in. (52 x 6 cm) wide.

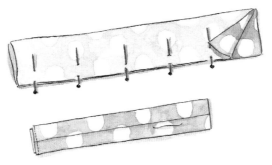

I Cut one 16¼ x 5½-in. (41 x 14-cm) and one 2⅜ x 11-in. (6 x 28-cm) rectangle of fabric. Fold the first piece in half, right sides together, and pin and machine stitch along the long raw edge. Turn right side out to form a tube and press, with the seam running down the middle of one side. Repeat with the second piece.

2 Cut a 6-in. (15-cm) length of elastic. Fasten a safety pin through one end and push it through the smaller tube. When the end of the elastic is in line with the end of the tube, machine stitch across both the tube and the elastic ⅜ in. (1 cm) from the end. Push the elastic through to the other end of the fabric tube, remove the safety pin, and machine stitch the elastic in place ⅜ in. (1 cm) from the end.

3 Place the large hairband piece on your work surface, seam side down. Line up one end with one end of the elasticated strip, and fold it over the elasticated strip. Machine stitch across the strip ⅜ in. (1 cm) from the end. Repeat at the other end and pull the main hairband over each end to finish.

BOW DECORATION

Cut a piece of fabric measuring 8³/₄ x 4 in. (22 x 10 cm). With right sides together, fold it in half. Machine stitch along the length and across one short end. Turn right side out and press. Turn the raw end to the inside, form into a loop, and secure with a few stitches.

Cut a piece of fabric measuring 3¹/₄ x 1³/₄ in. (8 x 4.5 cm) and again form it into a loop, as above. Press it and wrap it around the middle of the first loop, securing at the back with a few stitches. Stitch the bow to the hairband.

FLOWER DECORATION

Using the template on page 110, cut out four large flower shapes from a coordinating fabric and four small flower shapes from the main hairband fabric. Work a line of running stitch in a circle around the middle of each flower, gather to form a petal shape (see pages 106–7), and secure with a few stitches. Stitch the four large petals together to form the large flower and then sew the smaller ones in the center, finishing with a button covered in fabric.

Stitch the flower to the hairband.

BUTTON DECORATION

Cover a button in a scrap of fabric (see page 108) and stitch it onto the hairband.

Techniques

The sewing techniques used in this book are all very simple—ideal for quick-and-easy garments for fast-growing kids. You need only minimal equipment—sharp scissors for cutting fabric and thread, a selection of hand-sewing needles, tailor's chalk, some tracing paper, a pencil or fabric marker pen, and a basic sewing machine.

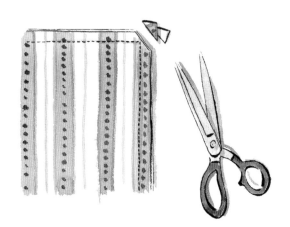

FABRICS

Most of the fabrics used in this book are dressweight cottons, which are available in a wide range of colors and patterns. Corduroys and denims are great for children's clothes, too, as they are very hard-wearing. Always pre-wash the fabrics (apart from wool fabrics) before you cut anything out to preshrink them, without using fabric softeners or conditioners. Dry and iron them before using them.

WORKING WITH PATTERNS

The patterns in this book are printed to their actual size. To use them, you will need to transfer them to pattern paper. Trace the patterns from the sheets at the back of the book onto tracing paper, greaseproof paper, or pattern paper, which is available from sewing and haberdashery stores. (Whatever you use, check that it is thin enough to see through.) Trace the pieces in the required size (the pattern guide shows you which line to follow) and cut them out.

Each pattern piece includes a seam allowance of $3/8$ in. (I cm). The seam allowance is the distance from the outer edge that indicates where the stitch line should be.

Lay the paper pattern on the fabric (fold the fabric if you need to cut two pieces), positioning it on the fold if necessary (the pattern will indicate this). Pin the pattern piece onto the fabric and draw around it with tailor's chalk. Remove the pattern piece and cut out the fabric pieces. Remember to flip the patterns over for projects that need a left- and a right-hand piece.

To transfer markings onto the fabric, slip a piece of carbon paper between the pattern piece and the fabric and run over the lines with a tracing wheel (also available from sewing and haberdashery stores).

ENLARGING MOTIFS TO THE REQUIRED SIZE

Some of the garments in this book have decorative motifs, such as the fruit designs on the Baby's bib (page 109–111); alternatively, you may decide to appliqué your own motifs. Although books and patterns often give motifs at actual size, it is useful to know how to enlarge them.

First, decide how big you want the motif to be on the finished garment. Let's say, for example, that you want a particular shape to be 4 in. (10 cm) tall.

Then measure the template that you are working from. Let's imagine that the template is smaller than the size you require—say, 2 in. (5 cm) tall.

Take the size that you want the motif to be (4 in./10 cm) and divide it by the actual size of the template (2 in./5 cm).

Multiply that figure by 100 and you get 200—so you need to enlarge the motif on a photocopier to 200%.

REDUCING MOTIFS TO THE REQUIRED SIZE

If you want a motif on the finished piece to be smaller than the template, the process is exactly the same. For example, if the template is 4 in. (10 cm) tall and you want the motif to be 2 in. (5 cm) tall, divide 2 in. (5 cm) by the actual size of the template (4 in./10 cm) and multiply by 100, which gives you a figure of 50. So the figure that you need to key in on the photocopier is 50%.

MAKING A TEMPLATE

To make a template for a fabric shape, first enlarge (or reduce) your chosen motif to the size you want.

I *Using a thick black pencil, trace the motif onto tracing paper.*

2 *Turn the tracing paper over, place it on card, and scribble over your drawn lines to transfer them to the card.*

3 *Finally, cut out the card shape using scissors or a craft knife on a cutting mat. You can now place the card template on your chosen fabric and draw around it with tailor's chalk or a fabric marker pencil to transfer the shape to the fabric.*

HAND STITCHES

These are the most common hand stitches used for joining (either temporarily or permanently) two pieces of fabric together.

BASTING (TACKING) STITCH

This stitch is used to temporarily hold pieces of fabric in place until they have been sewn together permanently. Basting stitches are removed once the permanent stitching is complete. It's a good idea to use a contrasting color of thread, so that you can see it easily.

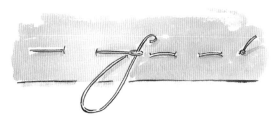

Knot the thread and work a long running stitch (see page 106) through all layers of fabric.

SLIPSTITCH

This stitch is almost invisible and is an easy method of hemming. It is also used to close openings—for example, when you've left a gap in a seam so that you can turn the garment right side out. Work from right to left.

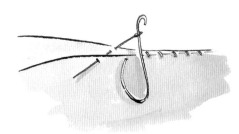

Slide the needle between the two pieces of fabric, bringing it out on the edge of the top fabric so that the knot in the thread is hidden between the two layers. Pick up one or two threads from the base fabric, then bring the needle up a short distance along, on the edge of the top fabric, and pull through. Repeat as required.

RUNNING STITCH

Running stitch is probably the simplest hand stitch of all. It is often used to gather a strip of fabric into a ruffle.

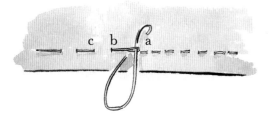

Work from right to left. Bring the needle up at (a) on the front of the fabric. Take it down again at (b), and up again at (c). Repeat as required.

MACHINE STITCHES

Machine stitching a garment together will make it much more hard-wearing and is obviously a much speedier method of sewing. A straight stitch is used to sew seams together. It is a good idea to sew a few stitches on an offcut of the fabric you are using to check the tension and stitch length.

ZIGZAG STITCH

This is useful for sewing along the raw edge of seams to neaten them off and prevent them from fraying. Use this stitch if you do not have an overlocking stitch on your machine. It is also used for sewing elastic onto the smock top (page 24), as it allows the elastic to stretch more than a straight stitch would.

OVERLOCKING.

Some machines have an overlocking stitch (separate overlocking machines are also available), which is used to neaten the edges of raw seams as above. It gives a very neat, professional finish.

CLIPPING CORNERS

At corners, it's a good idea to snip across the seam allowance to eliminate bulk and to achieve neat right angles when the item is turned right side out.

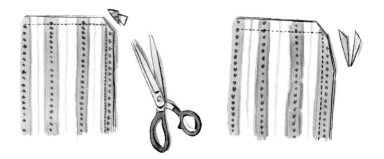

Simply snip diagonally across the seam allowance, making sure you do not cut through the stitching.

DOUBLE HEM

Double hemming gives a very neat finish and will prevent fraying.

Depending on the measurements specified in each project, fold the edge of the fabric over to the wrong side and press. Fold over again, pin, baste/tack, press, and machine stitch in place, stitching as close as possible to the folded edge.

GATHERING – BY HAND

Gathering fabric by hand is very easy to do—and on small items such as children's clothing, it is also very quick.

I *Take a needle and thread, and work running stitches along the edge to be gathered.*

2 *Gently pull the thread to gather the fabric to the required length, making sure the gathers are even. Secure with a few stitches at the end.*

BINDING

Binding is used to edge several projects in this book. To bind straight edges, strips of fabric cut on the straight of grain can be used. To bind curves, you will need to cut fabric strips on the bias:

1 *Using a square and chalk, mark lines about 1¹/₂ in. (4 cm) apart at a 45° angle across the fabric and cut along them.*

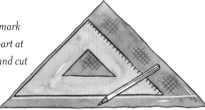

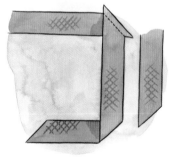

2 *To join strips together, pin and stitch the ends together along the straight edge. Press the seam open and trim the ends of the seams.*

3 *Continue to join the strips together until the bias strip is the required size for your project.*

MAKING A TIE

Several projects in this book require ties. There are two methods for making these.

METHOD 1

Cut a strip of fabric to the size specified. With right sides together, fold the strip in half along its length. Machine stitch along one short end and the long side. Trim the corners and turn right side out pushing the corners out neatly with something sharp (a knitting needle or a closed pair of scissors is ideal). Turn the open end in and slipstitch it closed.

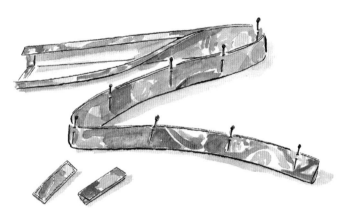

METHOD 2

For very thin ties (for a drawstring, for example), cut a strip of fabric four times the width of the tie required. Fold the short ends in to the wrong side by ³/₈ in. (1 cm) and press. Fold the strip in half along the length, press, and open out. Fold the raw edges in to this central fold, fold along the central fold again, pin, and machine stitch close to the edge.

MAKING AN ELASTICATED WAISTBAND

Elasticated waistbands are very easy to make and are great for children's clothes, as they are very easy to put on and take off. The same technique can be used for elasticating cuffs and ankles, as well.

I Turn 3/8 in. (1 cm) over to the wrong side around the top of the waist. Turn over again by the width that you would like the waistband to be and stitch in place, leaving a small opening. Topstitching around the top edge as well gives a nice, neat finish.

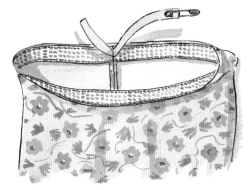

2 Attach a safety pin to the end of the elastic and thread it through the channel, passing it through the opening in the hem.

3 When the waist is the required size, machine stitch the ends of the elastic securely together and push them inside the channel. Slipstitch the opening closed.

SETTING IN SLEEVES

When sewing the sleeves onto the main body of a garment, you will need to ease the sleeve head around the curve of the armhole. Pin the arm in place and machine stitch in short sections, carefully easing the fabrics as you go to make a neat curve.

SELF-COVERING BUTTONS

Self-covering buttons are very easy do make and give a lovely tailored finish to a garment. The kits are available from haberdashery stores in a range of different sizes.

Cut a circle of fabric to the size indicated on the back of the kit, and pull it over the button front, securing it with the metal teeth on the back. Make sure that there are no creases in the fabric, then push the back of the button in place.

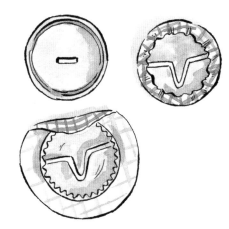

MACHINE-STITCHED BUTTONHOLES

Different sewing machines tend to use slightly different methods for stitching buttonholes, so follow the manufacturer's instructions for your machine.

I Mark the size of the required buttonhole on the fabric with tailor's chalk or similar.

2 Machine stitch a tight line of zigzag stitches along each side of the marked line, with a block of stitches at either end. Most sewing machines have a special buttonhole foot, which enables you to do this.

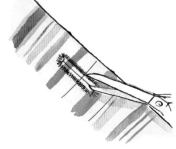

3 Using small, sharp scissors or a seam ripper, cut a slit between the lines of zigzag stitches.

Templates

These templates are full-size, so you won't need to enlarge them on a photocopier. The templates also include seam allowances where applicable.

Where a template is shown as a half, ensure you align the "center fold line" with the fold of a double layer of fabric before you cut out the shape. You could also fold your paper in half, trace off the template, then unfold it and pin it to your fabric.

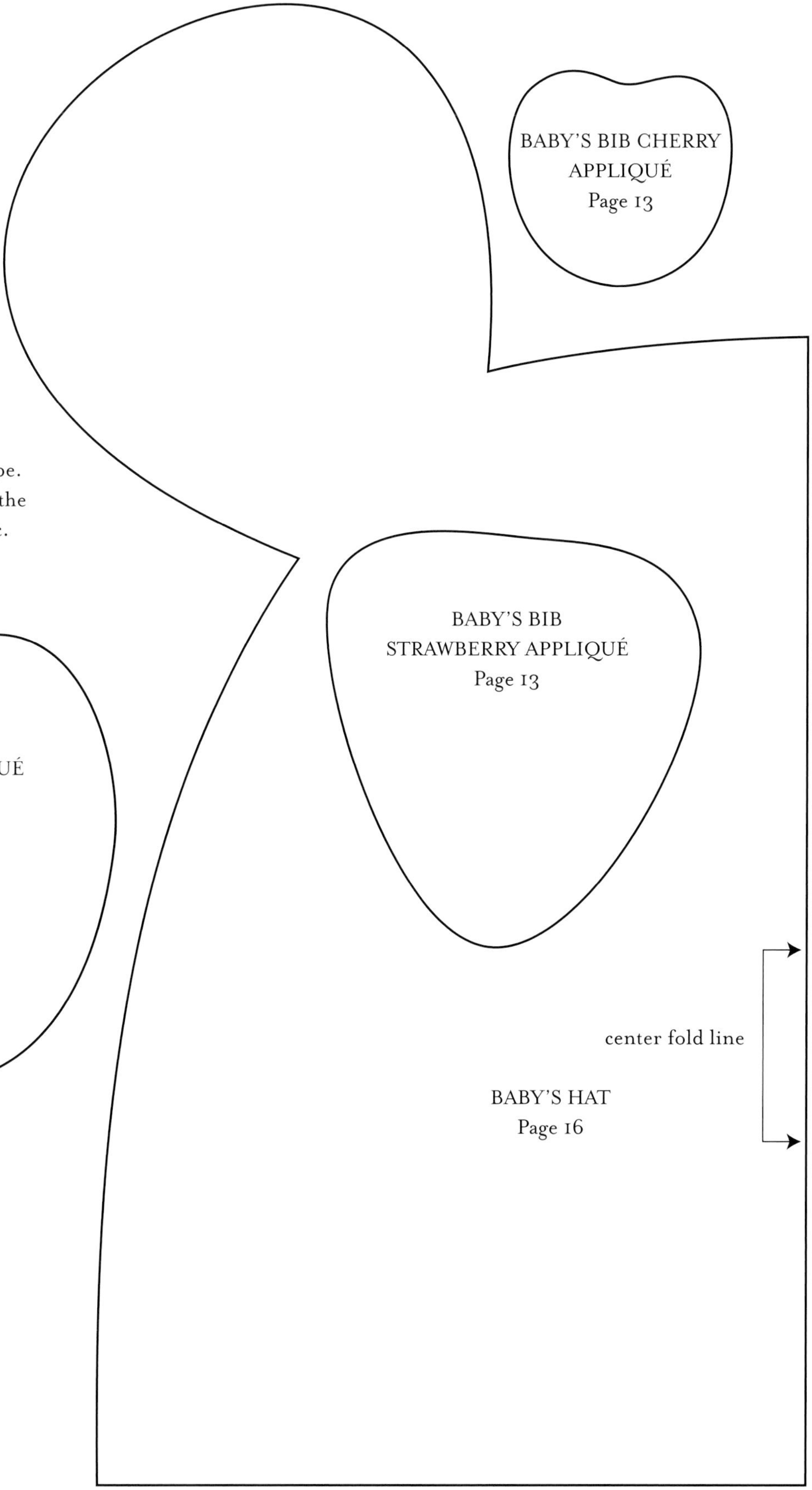

BABY'S BIB CHERRY
APPLIQUÉ
Page 13

BABY'S BIB
STRAWBERRY APPLIQUÉ
Page 13

BABY'S BIB APPLE APPLIQUÉ
Page 13

BABY'S BIB PEAR APPLIQUÉ
Page 13

center fold line

BABY'S HAT
Page 16

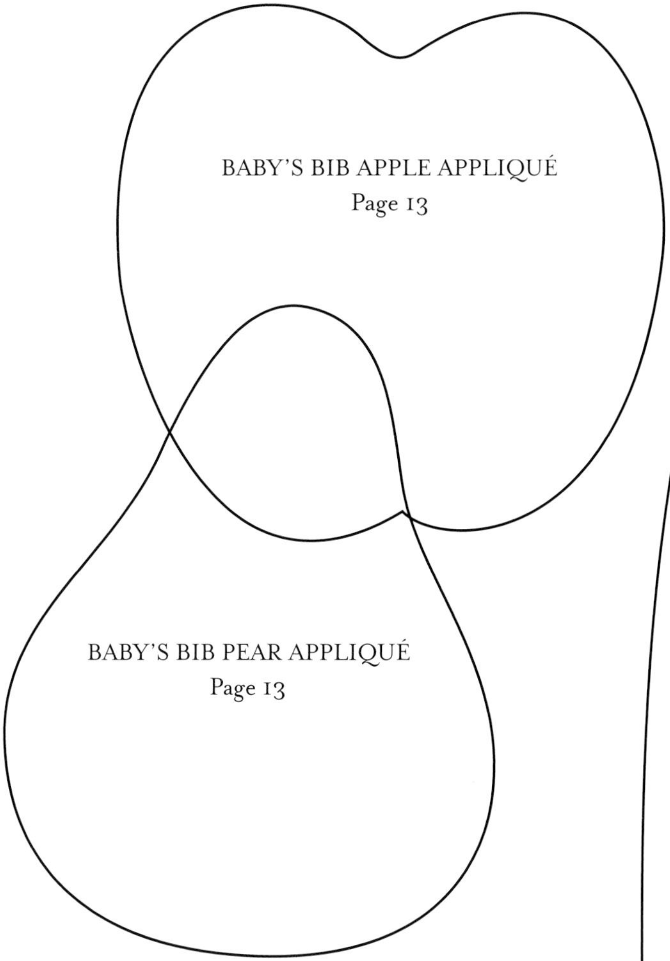

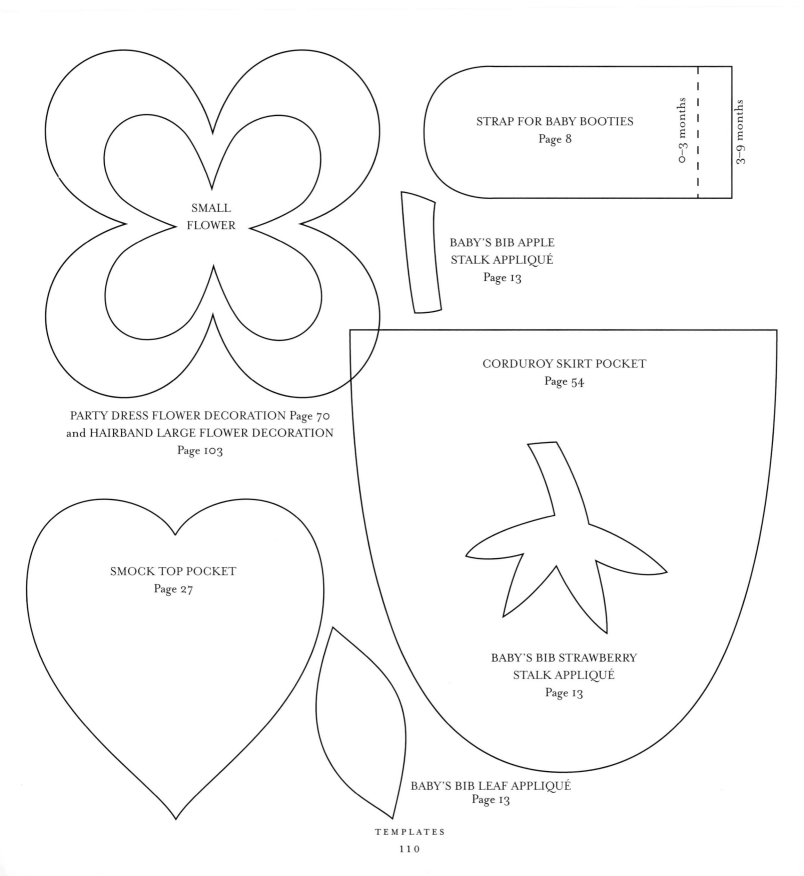

SMALL
FLOWER

PARTY DRESS FLOWER DECORATION Page 70
and HAIRBAND LARGE FLOWER DECORATION
Page 103

STRAP FOR BABY BOOTIES
Page 8

0–3 months

3–9 months

BABY'S BIB APPLE
STALK APPLIQUÉ
Page 13

CORDUROY SKIRT POCKET
Page 54

SMOCK TOP POCKET
Page 27

BABY'S BIB STRAWBERRY
STALK APPLIQUÉ
Page 13

BABY'S BIB LEAF APPLIQUÉ
Page 13

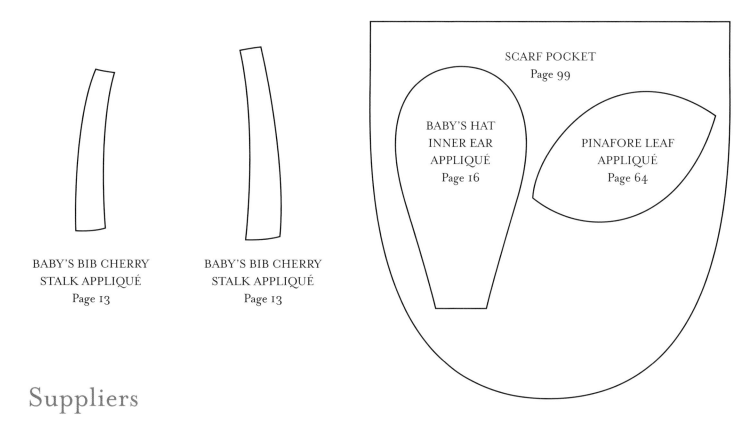

BABY'S BIB CHERRY
STALK APPLIQUÉ
Page 13

BABY'S BIB CHERRY
STALK APPLIQUÉ
Page 13

SCARF POCKET
Page 99

BABY'S HAT
INNER EAR
APPLIQUÉ
Page 16

PINAFORE LEAF
APPLIQUÉ
Page 64

Suppliers

US SUPPLIERS

Amy Butler
For stockists see
www.amybutlerdesign.com

Britex Fabrics
146 Geary Street
San Francisco
CA 94108
415-392 2910
www.britexfabrics.com

Cia's Palette
4155 Grand Ave S.
Minneapolis
MN 55409
612-823 5558
www.ciaspalette.com

Purl Patchwork
147 Sullivan Street
New York
NY 10012
212-420 8798
www.purlsoho.com

Reprodepot Fabrics
413-527 4047
www.reprodepotfabrics.com

Tinsel Trading Company
1 West 37th Street
New York
NY 10018
212-730 1030
www.tinseltrading.com

Z and S Fabrics
681 S. Muddy Creek Road
Denver
PA 17517
717-336 4026
www.zandsfabrics.com

UK SUPPLIERS

The Button Queen
76 Marylebone Lane
London W1U 2PR
020 7935 1505
www.thebuttonqueen.co.uk

Laura Ashley
0871 230 2301
www.lauraashley.com

John Lewis
Oxford Street
London W1A 1EX
020 7629 7711
www.johnlewis.com

Liberty
Regent Street
London W1B 5AH
020 7734 1234
www.liberty.co.uk

The Quilt Room
20 West Street
Dorking
Surrey RH4 1BL
01306 877307
www.quiltroom.co.uk

Stitch In Time
293 Sandycombe Road
Kew
Surrey TW9 3LU
020 8948 8462
www.stitchintimeuk.com

Ian Mankin
109 Regents Park Road
Primrose Hill
London NW1 8UR
020 7722 0997
www.ianmankin.com

The Cloth House
47 Berwick Street
London W1F 8SJ
020 7437 5155
www.clothhouse.com

Cath Kidston
08450 262 440
www.cathkidston.co.uk

VV Rouleaux
102 Marylebone Lane
London W1U 2QD
020 7224 5179
www.vvrouleaux.com

Index

apron 89–90

basting (tacking) stitch 105
bib, appliqué fruits 13–15,
    109, 110
binding 107
bloomers, baby 49–51
booties, baby 8–11
bows 29, 31, 59
    hairband 103
    making ties for 107
    tie 87, 90
buttonholes, machine-stitched
    108
buttons, hairband 103
    pockets 54–5
    scarf 97, 98
    self-covering 108
    snap fastener 101

corners, clipping 106

double hem 106
dresses, party 70–3
    pinafore 62–5
    toddler's 67–9
dressing gown 81–2

elasticating, technique 108

fabrics 104
flowers, appliqué 64, 110
    brooch 101
    corsage 21, 22–3, 69, 73
    hairband 103
fruits, appliqué 13–15, 109,
    110

gathering, by hand 106–7

hairband 102
    bow decoration 103
hand stitches 105–6
hat, double-sided 92–5
    with ears 16–19, 109
hem, double 106

machine stitches 106
buttonholes 108
motifs, enlarging 104–5
    reducing 105

nightdress 84–6

overlocking stitch 106

pajamas, 74–9
pants, capri 44–7
    elasticated 36–9
patterns, working with 104
pockets, button 54–5
    flap 42–3
    patch 27, 35, 36, 39
    templates 110, 111
poncho 100–1

rick-rack braid 49.50
rosettes 67
running stitch 106

scarf, appliqué 97–8
    pocket 99

shirt, boy's 32–5
shorts, boy's 41–3
size chart 7
skirts, corduroy 53–5
    gypsy 61
    puffball 56–9
sleeves, setting in 108
stalks, appliqué templates 110,
    111

tacking (basting) stitch 105
techniques 104–8
templates,
    appliqué fruits 109
    making 105
ties, making 107
tops, petal 20–3
    sleeveless 29–31
    smock 24–7

waistband, elasticated 108

zigzag stitch 106

HOW TO USE THE PULL-OUT PATTERNS—PLEASE READ CAREFULLY

The patterns in the pull-out section (opposite) are full size, so you do not need to enlarge them. It is best to copy the patterns onto tracing paper, parchment, or dressmaker's pattern paper and then cut out, that way they can be reused again and again. (Dressmaker's pattern paper or tracing paper is available from sewing stores or online suppliers.) The key shows which lines you need to follow for the different ages. Seam allowances are included where applicable; check the text for each project, as some measurements may vary. Also, check the pattern labeling carefully for special instructions, particularly on projects for babies and toddlers, to ensure you trace off the correct line that corresponds to your required age and size.

Some of the patterns are shown as halves. When you come to cut out these pieces of fabric, fold the material in half and align the CENTER FOLD LINE on the pattern with the fold in the fabric.

Where there are left and right sides to a garment piece—for example, the left and right front of a shirt—cut one side, then flip the pattern over before you pin it to the fabric and cut the second side.

Patterns 1–20 can be found on the first pull-out section and patterns 21–40 are on the second section.